Letting Go Love: A Love Story and Guide to Overcoming Self-Doubt

Copyright

2018 Elaine Walton

This book is dedicated to my first love; the One who inspired, encouraged and led me with His still small voice throughout the writing process. You are the One whom my soul loves.

Secondly, I'd like to thank my amazing husband and my family and friends for cheering me on throughout this process and loving me through thick and thin.

Special thanks go to Steve Omondi who took the beautiful photograph seen on the cover of the book; and special thanks to Sheree and Eva who so graciously edited this book with me.

With So Much Love,

Jeanette

Preface

But God chose what is foolish in the world to shame the wise; God chose what is weak in the world to shame the strong...- 1 Corinthians 1:27

Every person battles with insecurity at some point in their life. Some battle more than others, but nonetheless we all battle. I was one of those women who constantly battled self-defeating thoughts and insecurity. If you knew me you'd never believe it. I was so good at hiding behind perfectionism, but it got me nowhere. I was so insecure and afraid of what people would think of me that I very literally hid in a bathroom stall my first day of high school! And almost every day after that for an entire year I would hide during my lunch period. I wouldn't eat lunch in the cafeteria because I was so afraid of having conversations with people and not being interesting enough! Finally, I realized that I needed to let down my iron-clad walls of fear and insecurity and during the process I fell in love.

If you have ever been like I was, or you are battling self-defeating thoughts and insecurities, this book is for you. If you have ever felt so wrapped up in how you appear to other people that you lose yourself in the process, this book is for you.

We can become so engrossed in our façade that we forget to let our family, friends and even God in. This is a self-defeating process that hurts both you and the people you love most. My prayer is that this book will save many men and women from missing out on the blessings that God has for your life because you were clinging too tightly to this world and things like the following: **Fear, Insecurity, Perfectionism, Comparison (and Jealousy), Our (Unbending) Plans and Others' Expectations.** We will talk more about these six topics throughout the book.

The biblical account of Queen Esther overcoming her fear and insecurity encourages me. Esther was a Jewish woman in a Babylonian Empire who came to power through a mere beauty contest. During her reign as queen, there were some government officials who were set against her very existence. Her people group was looking into the face of death and only she had the authority to do anything for her people, God's people. She could have died in going to petition to her husband, the king, uninvited. Yet, with God's strength and "for such a time as this," she overcame great odds to save her entire people group.

I am sure Esther was not comfortable during this time of trial. The Bible makes it clear that she, along with her entire people group, fasted and prayed. Sometimes, God takes us to places that are very uncomfortable to stretch us farther than we could ever have imagined. He takes us to these places so that we can see our frailness and depend on His might.

Oh Adam, Oh Eve! How freeing it is to stand before the Almighty God unashamed; baring all of our shortcomings before a gracious and loving God.

Join me as I lay my and Evans's love story, my shortcomings and our victories before you, in the hopes of you learning from our story of pain, triumph and patience.

Please note that names were changed in this memoir to protect the privacy of each person mentioned. God is referred to using masculine pronouns to more easily reflect God as our father and Jesus as the bridegroom coming back for his church.

Blessings,

Jeanette Walton

And Moses said to the people, "Fear not, stand firm, and see the salvation of the Lord, which he will work for you today. For the Egyptians whom you see today, you shall never see again. The Lord will fight for you, and you only have to be silent." - Exodus 14:13-14

Chapter 1

Letting Go of the "Typical Love Story"

What is my strength that I should wait? And what is my end, that I should be patient? – Job 6:11

This is not your typical love story. This story will make you cry before you laugh and just when you feel you can't laugh anymore it makes you cry again. But, I hope it ends well. My prayer is that it ends well. I'm not sure how it ends... I'm writing it as its happening, which may or may not be the best way to write a love story. I think things are looking up.

It's not the fairytale or perfect love story like we all hope ours will be. I had such childlike dreams of what my future courtship would be like and it has been none of those things.

I didn't expect to date long-distance for three and a half years, going a span of two whole years without seeing my fiancé in person. And I certainly didn't know my husband would have experienced extreme poverty as a child. However, placing us together was God's planning, not mine. And I believe that God is showing me how to love beyond myself; that He is healing broken places in both me and within Evans through placing us together.

God wrote our love story. It was difficult to grasp God's goodness during all of it, but through everything, we had to trust that God was…and still is... good and He works all things for our good (Romans 8:28). It's better to go through life trusting God and receiving His peace rather than not trusting Him and living in constant worry when things do not go according to our plans.

Life is what happens, not what we plan. God changed my plans and allowed me to let go of Evans physically so that separately we both could grow more in love with Jesus Christ. Having to let go of the romantic fairytale in my mind forced me to hold tighter to my faith. No longer do I daydream about and idolize romantic love. I now think more about Christ Jesus and His great Love for me.

*Finally, brothers and sisters, **whatever is true**, **whatever is noble**, **whatever** is right, **whatever** is pure, **whatever** is lovely, **whatever** is admirable — if anything is excellent or praiseworthy — think about such things and the God of peace will be with you.* - Philippians 4:8

Chapter 2

Defeating Self-Doubt: Let Go of Your Ideals of "Perfection"

The previous chapter discusses how I had to let go of my perfect idea of a love story. Many times (in my own life at least) I strive for perfection, just to come back to the realization of my own weaknesses and great need to depend on my Father's strength.

"… 'my grace is sufficient for you, for my power is made perfect in weakness.' Therefore, I will boast all the more gladly of my weaknesses, so that the power of Christ may rest upon me."- 2 Corinthians 12:9

God's grace is the key; if we were perfect or could do things perfectly we would not need to rely on God's phenomenal grace. We have the great opportunity to love God with our whole heart and to serve Him with our life. We've been gifted with the beautiful chance to be used by a Holy, Righteous and Majestic God so that lives come to the knowledge of Christ Jesus. How awesome is that?!

But perfectionism comes from a deep desire to completely control what happens in and around our lives. However, as many of us "reformed-perfectionists" know, that level of control is just not possible. We can't control everything that happens; we can only control our response.

Sometimes when we are insecure we try to control our lives so that it seems like we are secure to other people.

Will we melt down, become enraged, complain, throw a fit or a temper tantrum when things don't go as planned? Or will we respond peacefully, with wisdom, tact and dignity? The choice is up to us. I'll come back to this specific topic with a few tips after we jump into some chapters.

Chapter 3

The Phone Call that Changed Everything

I will rise now and go about the city, in the streets and in the squares; I will seek him whom my soul loves [...] -
Song of Solomon 3:2a

Michael: "The airport is not too difficult to navigate. Just look like you know what you are doing. You are going to love Ghana. I miss it; I want to take my fiancé there [...] just enjoy your time. How long are you staying [...] Two months, wow you are really going to enjoy it! Have a safe trip. Oh, **and when you see Evans give him a big hug for me!**"

Me: "Okay, I will. Thank you so much for your advice!"

"...Oh, and when you see Evans give him a big hug for me!"

- May 18, 2013

-CLICK-

They say people tend to remember the beginning and the end of a conversation. So those fateful last words are ones which you didn't forget.

If the request for you to give some random man a hug, if you met him while in Ghana (because he was friends with your brother-in-law's cousin) sounds strange it's because it is. But I think it was God's divine leading.

That strange request was one of the few things that you actually recall from that fateful phone conversation with Michael. Yes, it is peculiar, but you promised to give some man named "Evans" a hug in Ghana, so by golly you would!

You think back to your parents' sweet goodbye at the airport in New York before you left for Ghana.

Your dad's cautionary remarks, "Now Jeanette, don't be like Taken."

Taken, you know, the action movie in which two teenage girls travel abroad and are taken captive.

"Daddy, I will be fine!"

You think about your mother's warm goodbye embrace and sweet words, "Jeanette, do you have everything? You need to eat something while you are waiting in the airport and remember that article you read about talking to strangers. Remember to walk around on the plane; you don't want to get blood clots. Baby…I love you, let me know as soon as you land. I love you."

When you arrived in Ghana you were introduced to the Mensahs, the missionary family you would be staying with. And within the hour you met Evans.

When you first met in Ghana, you knew he was special; but you were too prideful to admit it at the beginning. You felt the connection from the moment you hugged, but after you hugged it seemed like he didn't want to talk to you. When you tried to ask questions, he replied with short responses, and finally he left the room.

Yep, you remember that first day. DSTV in Ghana was showing a romantic comedy. You met and went to the living room and continued watching this movie. You remember eyeing Evans to see how he responded to the movie and questioning him and his best friend Scott.

"How long have you all been in Accra? What do you do?"

Upon hearing their answers, you summed up that Scott had come back to Ghana after his university studies in the United States. He had worked with leadership development and youth programs in Nkwanta, Ghana, and this was the end of his year there because he was enrolling in a seminary in Colorado in August.

Then you looked to Evans and asked, "What about you? What do you do?" He looked baffled:

"I'm finishing up university in Kenya, I actually came back to Ghana because I wanted to work with another nonprofit organization, but I didn't receive acceptance. So now I'm helping the Mensahs this summer." After this painful answer, for it seemed like he was extremely uncomfortable giving it, he promptly exited the room.

So, then it was just you and Scott…watching a romantic movie…which was weird. You broke the awkwardness:

"Hey Scott, is it okay if we tour the city? I'm so ready to see Ghana! I've been sitting on the plane for 10 hours and I don't want to just sit here!"

Anxious for a way out, Scott agreed: "Sure, let me go ask Evans if he wants to come."

He said this to your dismay. Evans was acting weird, and he seemed a bit awkward. You'd rather just go with Scott…but Evans agreed and you went on your first walk around Accra. You were mesmerized. Your heart was stolen by this beautiful, broken city. It was beautiful because of the many high-rise structures, the wealth of the people, and the people who welcomed you and who reminded you of home. It seemed broken because of the many unfinished buildings and dilapidated structures within the city.

The entire time you wandered the city (actually you only roamed the Cantonments area so you really hadn't seen anything yet!), Scott stayed beside you, describing structures, why people did what they did, and customs and language. Oddly enough Evans just hung behind.

You were irritated with this man, who obviously didn't want to be walking with you, and you finally looked behind you and said, "Are you okay? You're way back there; don't you want to walk with us?" Evans immediately looked up at you and sped up a bit to catch up.

Chapter 4

Defeating Self-Doubt: Tips for Letting Go of Perfectionism

Therefore, I tell you, do not be anxious about your life...
- Matthew 6:25a

In order to have our thoughts unclouded we have to let go of our ideal of perfection, or what we think is the "right way." Especially if our ideal of perfection is not reflected in God's word. Our love story definitely did not begin perfectly, as you can see in the previous chapter. Our story wasn't fun but it was God's perfect plan. The next chapters discuss more about our love story.

Friend, I want you to know that God's plan no matter how difficult it may be, is *the* perfect plan for your life.

However, God doesn't cause pain in our life. Our sin, temptation, and the effects of original sin cause pain in our lives. But, God can use those painful situations and *still* work everything for our good. How awesome is that!

   1.) It is imperative for us to **remember that we must honor God and seek His kingdom above anything or anyone else** in our lives (Matthew 6:33). Yes, your family, friends, and even society may say you should do something a certain way. Much of my tendency towards

16

perfection was fueled by an ungodly motivation to make my parents proud. However, I had to come to the realization that perfection was becoming an idol in my life.

2.) **Give it (your perfectionism) to the Lord.** Sometimes we get so wrapped up in our problems that we forget that God is bigger than our problems. Remember that the prayers of the righteous have great power (James 5:16). Remember that God is your helper and your comforter (2 Corinthians 1:3-7). God has your best God-honoring life already planned out and all you need to do is walk in obedience. Give God your perfectionism, lay it down at His feet and ask Him to help you let go of perfectionism.

3.) **Realize that as a child of God, who is obeying God daily, you can make no wrong turns.** God really does work everything for your good when you are called according to His purpose (Romans 8:28). Whatever direction you take, God will...GOD WILL... work it out for your good if you are trying your best to fulfill what He has called you to do. Even if you are afraid of messing everything up and even if things end up not being what you imagined as "perfect," **God will literally do**

everything to work it for your ultimate good when He knows you have a genuine heart of obedience.

4.) **Use Jesus as your measuring stick, NOT other people.** I used to compare myself to other people and gloat over how my actions "seemed" better than theirs. I thought I was close to perfect, but then I heard a pastor preach about how we as Christians should measure our lives to Jesus and realize how much we need His help and His grace. So as difficult as it may be, I encourage you to begin reading about the life of Jesus. You will soon realize just how far you fall short by comparison. When you stay in a place of humility before God, you will better overcome your perfectionism.

Chapter 5

Drawing Quick Conclusions

I was growing frustrated by this African man who I deemed was standoffish because he believed he was "too good" to talk to a woman. I had so many negative associations with African men, and I believed Evans embodied them all. Yes, he was probably chauvinistic, dominant, selfish, and self-absorbed like all the other African men I had met in college. This mindset was actually me just grieving over a crush I had on a few African guys who didn't "like me back" in high school and in college. I actually got stood up by a guy in high school who told me we were going to ice cream for a date...but never showed up. After my 16-year-old broken heart mended from being stood up, I prayed that the man who God presented as my future husband would take me out to ice cream (without me asking) on the first date. I concluded that that was how I would know he was going to be my husband. I prayed this prayer for almost four years before I actually met the man who took me out to ice cream (without me asking) on the first date.

After our 40-minute walking tour of Cantonments, Accra we headed back to the friend's house we were staying in so that we could go to the airport to meet the mission team coming in from Houston, Texas (boy oh boy, I didn't know what was in store!). But, first we went out to eat, which was a whole debacle in itself. Chinese restaurants are a delicacy in Ghana, simply because there are many Chinese businessmen there! So surprisingly the Chinese food in Ghana is pretty authentic. Scott, Evans, and Scott's parents Mr. and Mrs. Mensah all decided they wanted to treat me to Chinese. There we were... having a nice dinner, but Evans was still acting standoffish. After some awkward silences, with me attempting to get Evans to talk, Mr. Mensah finally spoke up, "Evans you've been acting strange ever since Jeanette came." I almost choked on the water I was drinking.

Could this man actually...like me? The thought crossed my mind for a split second, but I shot it down. I chuckled to myself, thinking: *No good looking, God fearing man, who I actually found attractive, has ever liked me. My "luck" probably hasn't and won't change, even if I am in Ghana.*

Now, you have to understand my past to understand my response. I had never had a boyfriend...NEVER. All the guys that asked me out stood me up at ice cream shops (lol). I wasn't really aware that I was a beautiful woman. I wasn't aware that anyone could love me in a romantic way, because all romantic love ever did for me was leave me with heartache, tears, and a lot of pain. After this comment made by Mr. Mensah I tried to shut Evans out of my mind. I closed myself off to him and stopped trying to ask him questions; I didn't want to get hurt...again.

Chapter 6

Defeating Self-Doubt: Letting Go of Insecurity

As you can see, I definitely struggled with self-defeating thoughts. I thought no man would ever want to marry me. Self-defeating thoughts, a lack of confidence, timidity: no matter the name you give it, insecurity will hinder your growth. When hidden behind clouds of self-doubt you may experience confusion and frustration.

Confusion comes in when you begin doubting what next steps you should take in your life. This doubt becomes overwhelming during times when you must make life-impacting changes. These changes could range from choosing a university to attend, choosing a major, buying a house, choosing a career, deciding on what jobs to apply to, deciding whether or not to move to a different location etc.

I've had many a season where my own doubt in my potential and God's word caused me to feel worthless, or like I didn't belong in a place I rightfully entered. Insecurity crippled me from making friends in high school and university and hindered me from being the most genuine version of me to other people. I felt like I wasn't worth anyone's time. I felt that I wasn't smart enough, interesting enough, pretty enough, skinny enough, and the list continued. Those thoughts caused me to figuratively pull out of the race before it began. I would also disqualify myself from being friends with certain people because I thought they were somehow "better" than I was. This was certainly a hindrance when it pertained to relating with people I was attracted to.

I was so scared that men wouldn't like me that I gave up trying. *By the age of 18 I had already concluded that I would never get married.* This was one thought that could have caused me to miss out on God's best for my life.

Thankfully, God intervened in ways that I never thought possible. I learned a few lessons along the way, and I'm excited to share them with you!

Chapter 7

Defeating Self-Doubt: Tips for Letting Go of Insecurity

I'll briefly discuss some of the steps you can take to help you to overcome insecurity. I'm praying that this advice will assist you in your journey:

1.) **The Right Outcome is Already Yours:** Once I realized what the Bible said about children of God, I realized that I didn't have to walk in doubt. You see, I doubted myself because I was ultimately afraid of messing up and getting hurt by people or circumstances. However, when you realize that *Jeramiah 29:11 "For I know the plans that I have for you, plans to prosper you, and give you a hope and a future,"* also pertains to your life, then you can walk with greater confidence. If you are prayerful, and following after God with all of your heart then God will "direct your steps" (Proverbs 16:9). God really loves you! God wants to see you succeed, and he will bring the right people into your life at the right time. No need to worry about being rejected by certain people or in certain situations. Be strong and know that God is with you (Joshua 1:9) and even if you face rejection, then those people just weren't meant to be in your life at that time. And you can trust that God is working things for your good when you set your relationship with Him as the priority.

2.) **Remind Yourself of Who You Are (even if you don't believe it yet):** I remember constantly telling myself that I was beautiful, I was worthwhile, and I was God's daughter. I would say all of these things to myself daily until I began to believe them. Remember to remind yourself that you are handsome or beautiful. Remind yourself that you are God's workmanship (Ephesians 2:10). You are a prince or princess in the eyes of God. You are worthwhile, and you are worth loving.

3.) **Always Graciously Accept Compliments People Give (especially about your character or talents):** Okay, Okay, I know this one sounds a little strange. But trust me, it works. I realized that when I was at my lowest point and people would give me compliments, I would always deflect the compliment. I would always say, "no, not me," or I would laugh it off. I did not know how to process praise because my thoughts about myself were so awful.

When people give you a compliment about your character or talents, always think about what the person said, and say thank you.

Just accept the compliment, and your brain will start to believe it and register it. People would tell me, "Wow, you have such a pretty voice," or "You're so sweet!" And I regret not being able to accept their compliments. I would constantly deflect the praise I was given.

This was my way of having a false sense of "humility," but actually it just pushed people away and allowed me to continue wallowing in my self-doubt (and lack of confidence). I vividly remember beating myself up after singing for worship service on Wednesdays at my college. People would tell me I did well, but I was so busy critiquing myself that I couldn't accept and reflect on the good things that they were actually saying about me. So please, do yourself a favor and reflect on the good things people say, and always accept their praise and say thank you.

These were a few things I did and continue to do to overcome insecurity.

Chapter 8

A Buffet of Bachelors

I was content being single. Have you ever felt this way too? It had taken me awhile to get to this place, but I no longer felt like I needed a boyfriend. My relationship with God was growing and developing, I was figuring out how I studied best in college, and I was finally content with the friendships I was making. I didn't feel the desire for a boyfriend like I had in the past. But God tested me during the summer of 2013 while I was in Ghana.

When we left that Chinese restaurant, we drove to the Kotoko airport in Accra to wait for the mission team from Houston.

I am very efficient at making lists. It may sound strange…and definitely had something to do with my tendency towards perfection in the past, but I did a mental checklist… or assessment of each single guy I met to rule them out of being a potential spouse (which I now know is silly, *and* self-absorbed). You can totally judge me, but I am just being truthful!

And of course, at the time I didn't really think about if those "bachelors" would also like me back!

I'd never met a man who even came close to my mental checklist of "perfect" qualities. Therefore, I didn't have "crushes" or people I liked from a distance anymore because I would always rule them

26

out. This list idea was how I protected my heart (no matter how strange the concept sounds) for my future husband. However, this summer was the test of a lifetime. Because little did I know while joking around and snapping silly photos in the airport, that the team coming from Houston, TX was a completely male team...with two married pastors and three single college age guys who were all solid Christian men! In total that summer I lived in the same mission house with FIVE bachelors. I was shocked! They were all good looking, and all loved mission work!

At that point I started asking God questions: *"Lord is this some kind of test?"* I honestly didn't know what to do with myself! I started trying to cross each of them off of my mental "LIST." I knew that they were not my main focus: teaching junior high school students in a small town in Ghana was my mission. Therefore, I wanted to quickly "cross them off" so I could focus on teaching (lolz).

I decided to do my own detective work. First, there were the two married pastors. They could give me information about the church they came from, whether the guys were being discipled, and any other background details.

This was helpful because I knew I wanted to be a missionary and I hoped to marry a full-time missionary or pastor. That alone ruled out two of the guys on the Houston team. There were only three left

(Evans, Scott, and one of the college guys on the Houston team). I also knew I wanted to marry a man who was a little older than me. This ruled out the last college guy. The only two left were Scott...and Evans.

After we collected all the guys from the airport, we drove them to the guesthouse they would stay in for the night, and we went to sleep in our respective rooms as well. I remember journaling that first night in a new country alone.

Despite being alone, I felt God's presence so heavy in that little room. I heard His voice whispering sweet securities over me, telling me it would be alright, and that he'd never leave me nor forsake me. Then I remember gazing around the room. The girl in the pictures was a family friend of Evans and the Mensahs. Her name was Lauren...I looked at her pictures with friends and thought about mine back at home. Would I grow homesick? What was the *real* reason I was here in Ghana? What was God doing? I had a sense of heavy expectation while in that room. I knew God was up to something...I just didn't know what.

Chapter 9

Flash Forward: Letting Go Love

For everything there is a season, and a time for every matter under heaven –Ecclesiastes 3:1

You glance back while waiting in the airport line. Thinking to yourself, *this cannot be real.*

A man in uniform tells you to open your suitcase, while he looks inside to do some sort of inspection. After a brief glance and his moving around of a few pieces of your clothing he says it's alright and you close it again.

Your eyes search for the white shirt. The shirt that buttons down, it's slightly wrinkled, but unsoiled…your heart feels like it's going to jump out of your chest and play hopscotch with your tears.

You're hoping that they haven't kicked Evans out of the airport yet. You wanted to say goodbye. A rock starts to form in your throat as your eyes frantically search. When you exit the line, you feel abandoned by the only man that you have ever loved in this way. Until you hear his voice,

"J, Hey J I'm here. I'm still here."

The panic subsides and you try to collect yourself, pretending that you were not panicking 30 seconds before you heard his voice. We walk together in silence, confidently so that the airport officials think we are a couple traveling together. We take heavy steps until we get to the escalator.

"Will they allow you upstairs?"

He shrugs his broad shoulders, "We can try."

At the top of the escalator there is an area for filling out the immigration card to present to customs. You become nervous when you can't find the card you filled out hours before. After a search that feels like eons you just decide to fill out another one. He patiently waits as you ask people to borrow a pen. One lady around forty with carefully manicured nails and a perfectly manicured smile finally loans you her pen, and you methodically fill the card out. You want to write slowly, slow enough so that you miss your flight home, and get to stay with this man, in this country forever. But the woman who loaned you her pen is eying you up and down, clicking her manicured nails. After you finish the card, we look at each other. You feel relaxed enough to just stare at his face.

The comfort you have with him is unlike anything You've ever felt before. It's okay to just stare quietly at the curves of his face and the sweat accumulating on his brow. He never tried to make advances;

we never kissed, for all of two months we just talked with each other. He spoke to you like a still small voice calling you home.

You had something for him. You begin removing sticky notes and markers from the Bible that you are holding, the Bible that you had been carrying throughout this entire trip to Ghana. The Bible you cried over, prayed with, and studied with for years before you'd met him. You handed him the brown leather-bound Bible.

"I want you to hold on to this and keep it safe. I will come back for it...I promise."

"No, J, it's yours"

"Evans, keep it. Please, please just keep it. I will come back for it and for you. I promise."

He nodded and we walk towards the escalator.

You hug his limp body goodbye. His body trembles and heaves, and then finally he returns the hug. It was an embrace in which all uncertainty lied. You did not know when you would see him again. You did not know where or how long it will be until he would be able to hold you again. We did not speak…every unspoken "I love you" was embodied in that lingering hug.

Then you let go…you let go of your love, to come home…or to someplace like home. They say home is where the heart is. If that is true…then your home like your heart is divided. You now have two homes.

Chapter 10

On the Road to Nkwanta

Beloved, do not be surprised at the fiery trial when it comes upon you to test you, as though something strange were happening to you. – 1 Peter 4:12

The next day we woke up and left the house before 6:30am, picked the mission team up by 7:30am, and we were on the road by 9am (after a brief stop to buy gasoline for the car and some other items). Finally, we began our seven-hour journey to Nkwanta.

Nkwanta is a small town in the Volta region of Ghana. It's a town that is rapidly growing because of its location, but it was also where the Mensah's house was located. I would be spending my summer (two months) staying in their house in Nkwanta and honestly, I just prayed it wasn't a mud hut.

The trip up was rough, physically and mentally. Every pothole led to physical discomfort, and every conversation with one of the five guys made me to feel a bit awkward. I didn't really know how to talk with guys. How was I going to navigate being the only single female in a house full of men for the next two weeks? I grew up with mostly sisters, so I had no idea how to interact with guys who I didn't really know. Eventually the guys fell asleep, and I could tell my heart to be still. I remember that long ride up, listening to a playlist on my phone and asking God to give me focus and clarity of mind.

On the way up we stopped a few times, and at about the second stop I had to use the restroom.

This posed a problem for me as an American woman. You see many restrooms in Ghana look much different than what we are accustomed to in the United States.

When we stopped at a gas station and I followed the signs to the women's restroom, I was in complete shock.

The restroom was outdoors with three walls just high enough to shield you if you were squatting. There was no toilet, just a rectangular trough (kind of like a pig's trough). I assumed this was what I was supposed to pee into because there was a hole in the middle of the low trough. It was a lot like a hole in the ground and the ground was sloped so the pee went down the hole.

I stared for a good 40 seconds (at least 40 seconds), and then I said to myself, "Jeanette, if you are going to be a foreign missionary, you are going to have to toughen up."

Luckily, I had some facial tissues stuffed in my bra. I don't normally stuff my bra with tissue, but I thought I may need them. My guess was correct. However, I didn't know what I would need them for!

So after I figured out how to squat without peeing on myself, I was well on my way to figuring everything else out...right?

After about six or seven minutes I came out from the walls and walked a few meters to our 16 passengers van and was greeted by the guys.

After we all got situated back into the van, we continued on to our destination. My head was swirling with ideas about what the village would look like as we passed through towns on the way. Oddly enough as we drove further and further away from Accra, the capital city, the more and more things started to feel familiar.

Growing up, my favorite place to be was outside on my family's farm. Our farm was a few hours away from our house. When we drove there I loved the freedom I felt by just staring into the vast ocean of corn, soybeans, tobacco and wheat, all growing in the fields. It always made me feel so much peace.

Life was a little slower on our farm and it always made me breathe a little easier. The farm was a place that seemed to never change. The stability it embodied breathed comfort over my little body like a quilt tucking a child in at night. Of course, nothing really stays static; places and people are always changing whether we see it or not.

As we passed through villages and towns, the life I saw gave me a sense of comfort, just as I'd had as a child on the farm. I felt so much peace as we passed women with mahogany skin and foreheads that glistened with perspiration from the heavy loads of fruit, firewood, and water on their heads. It was difficult to see children without shoes and with skimps of cloth for clothing, but the beauty was the strength despite poverty that I saw in the faces of children, women, and men.

The same determination was seen in the faces of my own family while they worked outside on the farm, and it was the same gritty determination I plastered on my own face when I was in school. I will make it. I can do it. I'd tell myself these words growing up in schools and in classes with people who didn't look like me or talk like my family talked. In school I used to tell myself I was an African Princess to keep from crying. Now, I finally was in Africa.

As we passed people and places, it was so familiar and yet so foreign. The people and the ocean of farmland reminded me of home, but the culture was so foreign. The whole time we were traveling I kept asking Scott, Evans's American "brother," questions about the culture. "Wow, what is that mountain called?" "Where are we now?" "How do you say that in the local language?"

I was fascinated with wanting to learn more and more about the culture of the people who looked so much like...my family. Scott and I grew close on that seven-hour ride to Nkwanta. We built an easy rapport, and I also talked quite a bit with the Pastor from Houston who was leading the mission team of college men.

Evans sat in the passenger seat up front and seemed not to notice or want to talk with me. I tried to ask him questions at first, but it seemed he wanted to have nothing to do with me. I assumed maybe he wanted to create a wall so that I wouldn't become attracted to him; you know how some young girls become enamored with men who are older or unavailable. It seemed he was trying extra hard to let me know he was not interested in me at all. So, I quickly received his message and left him alone completely.

I had no intention of "falling in love"... especially not with a man from Ghana. I had the wrong mindset that Ghanaian men were controlling, judgmental, and prideful, and those characteristics were not what I wanted in a man. So before coming I told myself I would absolutely not entertain thoughts of a relationship with anyone from there.

I continued to listen to worship music on my phone and tried to close my eyes and sleep at one point, but the road was just too littered with potholes. The van was jolting around and dodging to avoid holes in the road.

Chapter 11

Our Arrival

Humble yourselves, therefore under the mighty hand of God so that at the proper time he may exalt you -1Peter 5:6

It was around 6pm when we arrived. We passed construction vehicles lined on the road and I could see we were entering a little township.

One of the strangest things I noticed when we entered the town were the number of signs advertising local prayer camps. I soon learned from friends that these camps were "glorified" get-rich-quick schemes. The leaders of these camps made promises to deliver people from life's hardships and poverty by having them pay exorbitant amounts of money to attend. People were desperately searching for answers to heal life's woes and the supposed "men of God" were exploiting their poverty.

These types of advertisements are common in Ghana. There are a lot of people trying to make money off of the name of Jesus. And the sad part is...they are succeeding! In a subsequent trip to Ghana I even saw a "Fill My Cup Lord" Drinking Spot, aka a bar with a religious name to draw in customers. Everyone was trying to make money using religion. That billboard seen by all upon entering or leaving Nkwanta, allowed me to begin understanding just how open people here were to religion and how deeply people desired to know God.

When we entered the town the sun was setting, and my eyes tried desperately to take in everything that was around me. I saw a high volume of motorcycles and mopeds. I saw deserted construction equipment and soon learned they were working on the roads, especially the one main road. In this area I saw women carrying children tied securely on their backs with cloth. I saw elevated mountainous land to the north and east that I was told led to the next country over, Togo.

I took it all in, and it felt surreal. These were the things I'd dreamed about all my life. The images I'd longed to see and the areas I felt God was calling me to. This was so much more than I thought it would be. There was a weight of anticipation I felt about something God was going to do in my life while I was there those two months, but I didn't know what. "God, what are you up to? "

As we turned left off the main road and onto the secondary road that led to the hospital and to our house, I had to pinch myself a few times to make sure I was really there.

Chapter 12

My New Home?

Scott pointed to a few landmarks on the road we turned onto. The local hospital entrance to the right, a neighbor's house to the left and our house past the hospital.

When we arrived, a man who I later learned was Mr. Eric opened the gate that led from the road to the mission house which was on a little rocky hill. Mr. Eric was formerly a witch doctor but he had come to know the Lord through Pete and Linda Mensah. As we pulled up through the gate to the house, I noticed a metal gate beside the house behind which two dogs stood barking. To the left was what looked like a deserted brick building. I later learned that it was a mission library and Christian school that was being built on the land.

When we pulled into the driveway I heaved a sigh of relief and thanks to God. We made it safely to my new...home. We unloaded the car of its suitcases and walked into the mission house. Our shoes were dusty with red soil, so we kicked them off on the screened porch at the front of the house.

When I entered I was pleasantly surprised. I was prepared for mud huts and mosquito nets...but this, this was almost like any home you would see in the United States. There was an open living room and dining room as soon as you entered. A beautiful painting hung on the wall to the left in the foyer, underneath which was a keyboard. When I glanced to the right I saw wicker couches facing towards a TV in the far corner. For some reason I wasn't expecting that. Beside the television were a collection of DVDs and a book shelf of Christian Classics. When looking straight ahead I saw a large dining room table in the shape of an oval. It was covered in a beautiful African print tablecloth and had at least ten chairs that sat around it. Past the table to the left were the kitchen and a small laundry room.

When I went in the house I was in awe, I was excited, I was flooded with fear, I was eager with anticipation and questions about the students I would be teaching. So many emotions filled my heart. But of course, first things first. We had been on the road for seven hours and we had to eat.

That night Fati, the missionaries' cook, made rice, tomato-based stew, and a cabbage salad. After this meal, the guys helped clean the dishes (well we actually squabbled over who would clean them) because I wanted to help, but the guys from Texas were so sweet and wouldn't hear one word of it. They would clean and that was that. I just shook my head, smiled, and allowed myself to be led by Linda to my little room down the hallway.

The guys would all share two big rooms, and I got my own room, which was more like a suite with a bathroom attached. I guess there were some perks to being the only single female in the house!

When I walked in the room I felt nervous, because once again I was in someone else's room and I felt like I didn't belong. I saw pictures of a young boy with Scott and I assumed it was Pete and Linda's last son that I had yet to meet. I'd have to ask where he was at in the morning. The room was decorated so nicely and had a toilet! After my experience on the road, I realized that the toilet was all I *really* needed.

I prayed a little prayer of thanksgiving and asked for God's guidance as I would be here for two months, and I didn't really know what to expect. I wondered whether or not I should go back out to maybe say goodnight. After washing my face, and dressing for bed (I dressed modestly because there were so many single guys out there, five to be exact) I went back out to the living room and found the guys playing some sort of board game. I said a quick goodnight and shuffled back to my room. Before I completely shuffled away, Mrs. Mensah told me to be ready around 7am so they could take me to my school assignment.

I'd be teaching at a junior high school and I wasn't sure about any other information. I didn't know how many students I would have, I wasn't sure what grade they were in, or what grade level they would be on. I had no idea how school worked in another country and I knew the next day would be a crash course for me. I would need to learn as fast as I possibly could.

I woke in a cold sweat that first night.

It was all so vivid...*I was walking down the aisle to marry someone, but I didn't know who until I got to the end of the aisle.*

My heart was beating, my palms were sweating, but I somehow knew that this was the man God wanted me to marry. I had peace as I released my father's arm at the end of the aisle.

As my mystery suitor lifted my veil, I saw that it was..."EVANS!?"

I awoke suddenly and shook the dream off blaming it on the malaria medicine. The only odd part was that I'd been on the medicine for an entire week already and I hadn't had a dream until tonight. I was way too tired to ponder this, so I said a quick prayer and rolled back to sleep.

Chapter 13

First Day of School

For the sake of Christ, I am content with weaknesses, insults, hardships, persecutions, and calamities. For when I am weak, then I am strong.
– 2 Corinthians 12:10

The next morning, I lay in bed awake feeling first day of school jitters. Of course, this time it was a little different because now I was the teacher. I woke up with a strange awareness of being in a different country. Who was I here? How would the other teachers treat me? How would my students treat me? As the questions were racing through my head I finally just decided to cast my cares on Jesus because there was no use in worrying. I just knew that I would have to go...see... and learn as I went along.

I woke up before everyone else and I took a quick cold shower (because it was beyond hot to be this early in the morning). I picked out one of my favorite "teacher" dresses, put on a little makeup (to look older); I didn't do the greatest job with this task, and walked out of my room to take my malaria medicine with food.

I found a bit of bread and butter in the kitchen and drank a glass of water with my little meal. Then I waited...I wasn't sure what time school was supposed to start, but it seemed like I waited forever before people started waking up and taking showers. Linda and Pete came out first, greeting me and asking how I'd slept. They ate leisurely...and I felt like a coiled spring ready to burst.

When were we leaving? Would I be late? How far was the school? How many students did I have?

I just held my tongue and sat on all of these pretty critical questions (critical for me at least), as they slowly enjoyed breakfast. I knew that I had to trust them, and trust that they had a plan, even when I didn't know the plans they had for me yet.

This was the beginning of my three-year journey of learning how to let go of my plans and fully trust God's plans for my life, even when His plans didn't seem to "make sense," and even when it seemed like God took a little too long at the breakfast table that morning.

After they'd gotten dressed, we were off. I was mesmerized as we drove along; I took in new sights, sounds, and smells. People were up and about already! And it was only 8am.

It looked like rush hour, with women bustling with woven baskets on their heads, men glistening with sweat on their brows, and mopeds speeding in and out of the clusters of people on the road. To my eyes, it looked like utter chaos! But as time continued I'd learn to see order in this place I'd call home.

The road was dusty. I mean really, really dusty. You know the kind of red dust you only imagine in movies of faraway lands. Thick dust that coats everything including your nasal passages and makes your throat tingle. This dust flew up as we bumped along into town. A thick cloud of dust, like smoke, rose up behind our back wheels.

A part of me felt...embarrassed... riding around in this old Land Rover, because it seemed quite opulent. Few people actually had cars here, so this was very obviously a sign of great wealth. In the U.S. I wasn't rich...but here it seemed like we had a whole lot of money.

We continued straight along the main road, until we came to a ravine on the side of the road. On one side of the road was the orphanage, on the other side was one of the public junior high schools in the area. Pete stopped the car and jumped out; I hesitated, then joined him on the other side.

"This uh, is your school. We'll go in with you to talk with Headmaster Joseph. He knows you're coming, but you know here we have to introduce and recount what was said before, you'll see."

We walked up a little dusty red hill and I saw the school.

Chapter 14

Defeating Self-Doubt: Letting Go of Our (Unbending) Plans

The previous chapter mentions how I had to let go of the plans I had for what my internship at the school would look like. Releasing our plans to God may seem like a simple concept to talk about, but it's a very difficult one to live out. Letting go of your plans and submitting to God's plans for your life can be challenging. I know it sure was hard for me at least! However, we have to keep reminding ourselves of what it means to be a "Christian."

A Christian is a follower (or disciple) of Jesus. Being a follower of Jesus means letting go of your life (plans included) and trusting Him to lead you. Let God be the author of your life; that means constantly living a life where you submit EVERYTHING to Him.

Now I know that this can be scary but when you remember that God created you and knows exactly what you will be fulfilled in doing, then we can trust that whatever plans He has for us are so much better than anything we could have thought up for ourselves. Sometimes our natural, God-given inclinations will even lead us towards the plans that he has for our life. We'll talk more about this after the next few chapters.

Chapter 15

First Day of School

Surprisingly, the first thing I noticed about the school was not the school building itself. The first thing I noticed was the red dust. I'd never seen dirt look so…neat. The students swept the dusty grounds in front of the school every morning for their morning chores. My eyes were drawn to little rock paths in the red dust leading to the different blocks of classrooms. Children had on brown and golden-yellow school uniforms, a few were sweeping, some were walking here and there carrying chairs and desks to and from the classrooms.

It was hot. It was only 7am in the morning and already, it was hot. We walked up the red cinder block stairs to the building where the headmaster's office was located.

As we entered the room I heard the whirring of a fan and we experienced a bit of relief from the scorching morning sun inside the headmaster's dark office. I could see that he was a well-read man, as there were books lining the office floor. There were extra sets of primary books and extra English books, some were mathematics and science. His desk sat in the very center of the room. It was intimidating. But Mr. Mensah (my surrogate father for the time I was in Ghana) stepped up, introduced himself, recounted the details of my coming to work as a teacher's assistant there at Adome Model School, and then introduced me.

When Headmaster Joseph saw me, his stern countenance changed from rigid to soft. He smiled and shook my hand; of course, I smiled and thanked him for the great opportunity to teach at the school for a few months. These few words of thanks delighted the headmaster and he immediately took a liking to me, and I immediately liked him. He reminded me of a grandfatherly figure. He was soft spoken and stern, but deep down I could tell he had a heart of gold. He loved the children he was charged to educate, and he would do that with all that he had. Even if the resources he had to work with were very few.

At the end of the introduction, Headmaster Joseph called me daughter, and told Mr. Mensah he would take care of me while I was at the school.

Mr. Mensah left the school grounds, and I stayed with Headmaster Joseph, who then proceeded to take me on a tour of the school. There was a kindergarten, primary, and junior high school all on the school grounds. The kindergarten and primary school were on the far side of the grounds, and they were in the shape of a rectangle. The junior high school block of buildings created another neat little parallel rectangle to the primary school class buildings. The entire complex was set up as two parallel rectangles with a large courtyard in the middle of the rectangles.

The classrooms were "open concept classes," you could say. There were open windows with no glass, and open doors. So, anyone could walk by and hear what you were teaching at any time. After meeting all of the kindergarten, primary, and junior high school teachers that were there at that time, I finally met James. James was the teacher I'd be assisting while I was there.

Upon seeing him teach I was impressed by his command of the classroom. I realized that I could learn a lot from watching him teach and I was excited to get to help! James had about 70 students. Each of them was intently focused on what he was saying. Little did I know that some of the good discipline was due to the teachers legally being able to "cane" students, which is the equivalent to spanking the children.

I was never given a detailed list or schedule of the classes I was supposed to assist with. This was to my detriment until I asked a teacher friend to copy her school schedule. This helped me time my classes accordingly. I didn't know how important that schedule would be.

All of my co-workers (especially the men) were so welcoming to me. Many of the teachers had never talked with an African-

American person and I received questions about whether or not I knew President Obama, and where my parents were from. Many of the teachers were surprised by the fact that I didn't know what country my parents or grandparents came from. I literally had to explain my history using the slave trade in Africa as my reference point. I think that history was hard for many of them to hear. I had a few teachers who continued asking questions and a few who lost interest in me pretty quickly.

But everyone agreed…I looked like I was Ghanaian! Isaac, Ishmael, James, and Miriam all tried to guess what tribe my ancestors were probably from. Some said I looked Ewe, some said Ashanti, but all wanted me to be from their own tribe. Some of the liveliest conversations I had in Ghana were with my co-workers…friends that I made while teaching at Adome Model School. As the school day waned and came to an end, I was thoroughly exhausted and overjoyed to see Mr. Mensah's tan colored Land Rover pull up to the school grounds.

When I hopped in he asked if I was feeling up to going with the guys to a nearby village to help with a local church Vacation Bible School. How could I turn that offer down?

Chapter 16

Childhood Dreams...

However, as it is written: "What no eye has seen, what no ear has heard, and what no human mind has conceived" – the things God has prepared for those who love him—these are the things God has revealed to us by His Spirit. The Spirit searches all things, even the deep things of God.

– 1 Corinthians 2:9-10

When I was eleven I had a vivid dream that changed the trajectory of my life...

I was in a dry and red-dust covered place working with children.

The children were shades of dark coffee bean brown, and mocha colors, just like me.

But the little ones, even the girls, didn't have hair.

Why was their hair cut so short? Why was it so red and dusty?

The children flocked around the older version of me in the dream. I had on a long dress, and I knew that this was what God wanted me to do with my life. I knew that this was my life's calling.

Rarely do we have such clarity of calling in our lives, but there's something about the faith of a child genuinely asking God what He wanted her to do with her life. I now wonder if God had given me that dream when I was an adult would it have made such a serious impression upon me. I don't think it would have. I think I would have found some way to reason through it, logically dismiss it, or forget about it. But Oh, how beautiful is the faith of a child.

I believe God speaks to us clearly. He speaks in ways and at times where we will clearly hear Him. Yet sometimes, we are so busy and cluttered with headphones in, cellphones in hand, and constant stimulation that we miss His communication. If you want to know God's purpose for your life, I dare you to ask Him, and provide space for Him to respond. Take a week, put down your busyness, clutter, headphones, cellphones, and computers and get still and quiet before the Lord. Reflect on what you naturally like to do, and how those activities can enhance the kingdom of God.

I'd rather be called a "crazy person" for running after what I believe is God's purpose for my life, than to be a "sane" person working a nine to five job that God never told me to work. Now, if God is purposefully calling you to work that nine to five job and witness to your co-workers or reflect His love in other ways through your career then great! I had three jobs in college and I believe God intentionally placed me at two of those jobs to witness to my co-workers. One co-worker I shared with came into a right relationship with the Lord through that at that job.

Your life is seething with purpose. You've just got ask God for the clarity to know what that purpose is.

Whelp, that was a brief detour… I promise it will make more sense to you when you read the next chapter about Vacation Bible School in the village.

Chapter 17
Journey to Odumasi

Have you ever been so full of joy that you literally become speechless? Well that was my exact feeling after Vacation Bible School in the village. Although it was a rough ride to the village…for more reasons than one.

"So, Jeanette, what are you looking for in a man?" This was an awkwardly timed question for me. We (the three college aged guys from Texas, the two single missionary's sons Evans and Scott, the Mensahs, and the two mission chaperones) were all on our way to Odumasi, a small village just outside of town.

We were "conveniently" cramped all together in a tan Land Cruiser, being jostled along by the red dirt road rife with trenches, potholes, and gaping ditches. There was actually one point where we thought we'd have to get out and push the Cruiser out of a muddy ditch we'd landed in on the road. Our driver was doing the best he could, given the circumstances. But honestly, I didn't know whether we'd (or I'd) make it or not.

On the way, one of the mission chaperones for the college guys asked me the question, "What are you looking for in a man?" All eyes turned on me. All of these guys were single…and potential "suitors" …and I was the only single woman around until next week when another short-term mission intern was coming. I knew it was all fun and games, and this particular pastor really liked to play around and get the team to know one another better, but this question was really, really uncomfortable for me.

"Umm, well…I umm, I have a list of things I'd like in my future spouse, one big thing is that I'd like for him to be a pastor." Three of the guys were ruled out by this answer and only Scott and Evans remained in the "running" if you could call it that. I was attracted to Evans, but it seemed like he didn't notice me. From what I had gathered, Evans was pursuing a degree in theology and was a wonderful teacher and preacher. Scott was nice too and was going to seminary in the States next year…so logically it would make more sense to get to know him further…he wasn't my type physically, but he was handsome, so maybe if he showed interest, I'd get to know him more. Evans did not seem to be interested in me (which only bothered me a little bit), nor did he seem to want to be friends whatsoever. I figured if anything romantic was going to come out of this trip, it would rationally occur with Scott…right? Also, I wasn't there to go "husband hunting." I kept telling myself to push the feelings for Evans down because I was here to teach, and I was content being single.

As we pulled up to the outdoor church in the village, children began to gather around the familiar car. They knew this to be the Mensah's car, always bringing joy and new people to visit. This load didn't disappoint the children in the village. The college guys had a soccer ball! We were arranging for a soccer game to kick-off the week of Vacation Bible School. How fun it would be for the guys…but what would I do? I surely wasn't going to play soccer with the men in a dress.

As I was pondering this idea, a little girl who was about five or six years old walked up to me and tugged my dress with her little hand. I looked down at her big coffee colored eyes as she stared up at mine. She called me "Nana," which in the local language means princess. She thought I was beautiful. I had picked up a few words in broken Twi and I told her she was also beautiful. She smiled with glee (I'm not sure if it was because of my funny accent or my broken language) but she went to get her friends. The next thing I knew there were three pairs of coffee eyes gazing up at me. So, I got down on my knees and decided to play a hand clapping game similar to patty cake with the girls around me. To each girl I spoke the words, "You are beautiful." After a few minutes playing with them, they went to get more friends. After sometime there were about ten girls who joined the clapping game with me.

"Okay let's walk down to the field everyone!" I heard someone shouting these words. Everyone began coming out of houses and shanties and walked down towards the field. I had no idea where to go. But the first little girl grabbed my hand and gleefully began walking me down to wherever the soccer field was. Another girl grabbed my hand and began to escort me down. Then children came from all over and were following me; running, and prancing, and skipping all around.

It all just felt so surreal. By the time we reached the field there were close to thirty or forty children at my heels wanting my attention, hoping to play clapping games and hear the American lady tell them they were beautiful. There is something so pure and loving about the faith and friendship of a child.

It was at this time that someone from the mission had the children pose around me for a picture. So many beautiful ebony faces all smiling with joy at playing a little game. My heart felt like it would burst. I was so happy. In that moment I knew that I could stay here in northern Ghana for the rest of my life and be content.

The children began to disperse as the soccer game began. There were eleven men on our team and eleven men representing the village. The game was incredible to watch, the atmosphere teemed with excitement. We were all cheering and laughing. Euphoria filled the atmosphere. After the game (to this day I have no idea who won, this was my first time watching soccer) the guys announced that there would be Vacation Bible School for the next few days at the church, and people slowly dispersed.

One young man came up to me with camera in hand. "I thought you'd like to see this picture."

It was the picture of me with the children all around, but it triggered such a deep memory that I gasped. This picture was the exact image I'd seen in a dream I'd had eight years prior. The little girls' hair was shaved.

I managed to stutter, "Thank you...do you know why the girls have such short hair?"

"It's to show that the little ones are not of marriageable age, they only do this in northern Ghana."

"Oh, okay...thank you."

We piled slowly back into the Land Cruiser, the boys reeking with sweat. But it didn't bother me. Neither did the long bumpy drive back. I was so lost in thought that I wasn't really there. The picture...it was the same as my dream. *How was it the same as my dream?*

Chapter 18

Defeating Self-Doubt: Tips for Letting Go of Our Unbending Plans

1.) **Following Jesus means asking Him for directions, listening, and obeying His answers.** You can ask questions like: God, what do you want me to study, what do you want me to do for a living, God, do you want me to get married? Who is your best pick to be my husband? God, how many children? God, where do you want me to live? God, what do you want us to do while we live here? God, what do you want the mission of our marriage to be?

2.) Now you may be asking: "What if I can't hear God's voice?" That is when I'd encourage you to **get into your Bible and dig deep (study) before it is time to make a decision so that you get used to hearing His voice in the "seemingly" small areas of life.** Read His word and talk with Him every day. If you submit every day to Him before you have a big decision when the time comes for a decision to be made you will be saturated with His presence, and in His word and you'll know what steps to take. Those scriptures you memorized will start to overflow out of you and you will know. You'll either have peace about the decision or you won't.

And then when you are talking with Him on the daily and walking with Him, if you happen to make the "quote on quote" wrong decision God will still be with you. He knows you love Him and that you're seeking Him. He will still be able to accomplish the purposes that he has for your life because you have surrendered to Him completely and God abides in a surrendered heart that abides in Him (John 15:4).

By staying in His word and praying "without ceasing" we are reminding ourselves to submit to Him every day and with everything in our lives.

If you love me, keep my commandments- John 14:15

3.) Do you submit your will to Him? Do you let go of your plans for your life so that He can lead and plan your life? Or do you just drag Him along and pull out the Jesus card every now and then just to make sure you are going to heaven?

Salvation is not a one-time thing; many people think the story stops at the altar-call, but as humans we keep sinning and we need to keep confessing and turning back to God. Throughout our life we are in the process of sanctification (being made like Christ/being worked on and refined).

Your actions after your initial repentance and belief will show if you really believed, if you actually trusted God and genuinely wanted to get to know Him. The Bible should start to change how you walk and how you talk. It should change who you hang out with and you may be convicted about things you have never been convicted about before. Being a Christian means following Christ. You cannot follow Jesus without knowing what His Word says, and you cannot let go of your plans in a God-honoring way without fully following Jesus.

Chapter 19
Confirmation

"You may now kiss the bride." The Pastor spoke to the mysterious man in front of the entire audience of witnesses.

I was frantic. "Who am I marrying, excuse me…who am I…EVANS?!" The young man gently uncovered my white veil and leaned forward.

I woke up saying his name again in a cold sweat. What is going on here? First the picture and now I am having this crazy dream.

This must be a satanic attack. How else could I explain this colorful dream? I was marrying Evans? Do I even like Evans? He doesn't even talk to me…

"Lord, help me to focus on teaching my students. That's the real reason I'm here. Amen."

With that short prayer, I checked the hallway to make sure no one heard me saying Evans's name. After I was sure everyone was asleep and no one heard, I closed my door and crawled back underneath my sheets to go back to sleep; hopefully with no more strange dreams.

At school a few days later, headmaster Joseph delivered some grave news.

"Madam Janet, one of our teachers is leaving for distance learning classes for a few months. Therefore, James your head teacher is taking over her classes. You will take James's class for the time that you will be here."

My jaw dropped. I was going to have to teach a class of 70 sixth graders…in a different country…by myself?

"Yes, sir, umm, is there anything I should be helping them with?"

"James will tell you what the class has left to learn. You will begin teaching them today."

James stepped up and took out a Golden English Grammar book that the students were supposed to be learning from. He circled the units that needed to be covered while he was gone. I gulped a few times and tried to calm down.

"Don't worry, if they give you any trouble just tell me and I will use the cane on them. You are welcome to use it as well; these kids need to learn."

The cane was a strange practice to me. It was basically a form of public punishment involving the teachers literally spanking the students with a tree limb. I honestly couldn't watch as this corporal punishment took place. I would have no such dealings in my classroom. I would have to find other ways to reward and discipline my students.

I walked into the classroom I was to occupy, the nearest one to the library. I had a giddy excitement building in me, but also a fearsome nervousness. This is what I had come for. I quickly took out the emergency lesson plans I had (always be prepared); I knew I wanted to encourage my students to be all that they could be and try as hard as they could to attain their dreams.

The classroom had a musty smell. The colorful paint was chipping a bit, but I knew I wanted it to be a classroom full of joy. I wanted my students to leave my class everyday feeling excited about what their futures had to hold. There was a chalk board that covered one wall of the classroom about 12 feet wide and six feet high. Facing the board were about seventy wooden desks with long benches for seats. Some of the desks were wobbly, some were sturdy, and all would soon be supporting a child who hopefully wanted to learn.

As I gazed at my "open concept" classroom, the weight of the task felt heavy on my shoulders. I wanted these students to do well, but I felt like only a child myself. I knew I could do all things through Christ who strengthened me, so I swallowed hard and started to think about that day's lesson plans. I was thinking mostly on my feet, since I'd only had a few hours' notice that I'd be teaching the next few English classes.

When my students walked in, some giggled and looked away, some greeted me, some waited until the very last second to come in.

"Okay! Okay!" James's booming voice settled the students into their desks.

"This is Madam 'Janet,' she will be with you for a few weeks teaching English, I expect that you will give her your utmost respect..." At least that's basically how I remember him saying it, though I believe he probably said it with more flare. James was quite theatrical. He introduced me to the class and then he promptly left to teach his new class.

"Well, class my name is Madame Jeanette, and I am so glad to be with you all for these next few weeks! I am from the United States and I am excited to get to know where you are from. Now, I only have two rules and that is to respect me and to respect your classmates. When I am talking you should be listening. Now, I want to know a little bit about each of you, I'd like you to stand and say your name and your favorite food."

To this statement I was met with blank stares and squinted eyes. It seemed as if everyone in the class was staring very intensely at me trying to figure something out.

"We can start on this side of the room." I pointed to my left.

"What is your name, and your favorite food?"

I was pointing to a young boy who was maybe 15 or 16 years in age.

In Ghana you can have a wide range of ages in one class because many students wait until their family has the money to send them to school. This can leave teachers with some students being as old as 16-years in the sixth grade.

His petrified look made him look much younger though.

"Maaaammaadam, Madam, Pardon?"

This response was one I was not expecting.

"What do you mean 'pardon,' answer the question."

"Madam," I heard a timid voice speak up. It came from a small boy, he was smaller than all of the other students in the class, but he would prove to be one of the brightest students in my class.

"Madam, you are speaking very fast and we cannot understand your speaking."

I looked at him for a second, compassion and embarrassment filling my heart. The class couldn't understand my accent! I thought I had prepared for everything but this…this was hilarious to me.

I have an accent from the Southern United States. Some of these students could not understand my speech. So, I had to think on my feet and I decided to have that one child in the front repeat everything I said so that the class could understand. This took considerably more time, but at least I knew my students would be learning.

After Wisdom (I kid you not that was his name) finished translating my Southern English into Ghanaian English, every student stood and introduced themselves although some were shy at first. There was not a lot of deviation between the kids' favorite meals (fufu with light soup)…but it was a start.

I then introduced myself. "My name is Madame Jeanette, and my favorite food is spaghetti (which I had to explain to the class later), I love teaching and I am so glad to be here with you all."

"Madame, what tribe are you from?"

This question came from one of the faces looking up at me, I am not sure who, but I answered as best as I could.

"Well, I am Black American, I was born in America, and I have no tribe, but my people have a wonderful history of triumph despite hardships."

Another question squeaked out. "How do you not have a tribe? You are Ghanaian?"

I had to give an abbreviated version of my entire history, and it went a little like this:

"I am not sure where I am from. You see in my history, my ancestors were taken from here and other countries in Africa, like Nigeria, and Burkina Faso, then they were sold as slaves in America. So, my great-great grandparents were slaves and they had children, and they were not allowed to pass down language or information about what country they came from to their children. So, their children do not know. But, praise God my ancestors fought to be free from slavery, and oppression. And we have a man named Martin Luther King who also helped Black Americans be treated equally in America."

And then...the whopper of all questions came..." Who is Martin Luther King Jr.?"

I was in shock, but also realized that my history was not theirs. I quickly explained how Martin Luther King Jr. fought for the freedom of Black people in America.

Next, I asked the students to take out books to silently read (all of my speech was still being translated from English to English).

My students stared at me with blank stares…. they did not have books (other than the grammar book) to read.

I felt tears pushing the lids of my eyes…in the States we take our many books and libraries for granted, and these students did not even own one book at home. They told me they were not allowed to take books out of the school library, so all of their English reading and speaking practice came at school, or from any extra classes their teachers offered. My students were downcast when it was time to go, but I had one more thing I wanted them to do.

"Okay, class I know that it is almost time for you to leave but repeat after me, 'I know I can be what I want to be. If I work hard at it, I'll be where I want to be.'" This was the chorus of a rap song I'd once heard, and I felt it was fitting for my kids to say it until they believed it. Well…we actually rapped it, and my kids thought that was the funniest thing! After our class rap (that we ended up doing almost every day), the students were dismissed to go to their next class period.

Chapter 20

And Jealousy Crept In...

Thou shalt not covet thy neighbor's house, thou shalt not covet [...] anything that is thy neighbor's – Exodus 20:17

I came home exhausted that day; a teacher from school dropped me off at the mission house which the people in town affectionately referred to as "the white people's house." Even though we were Black Americans, we were still foreigners...the equivalent of white people in Ghana.

When I walked into the cool of the house, the guys invited me to do Vacation Bible School with them again and I politely declined. I just wanted to soak in everything that happened at school that day. I laid down on the couch in the living room and took a nice little nap. It was almost dark when I awoke. The guys were still gone but Fati was finishing dinner. I felt alone, but so perfectly in God's will.

I took out the small book bag I carried my school books and lesson plans in and began to plan for the next two weeks. The students were expected to know about Transitive and Intransitive Verbs, Identifying articles of speech, and Subject-Verb agreement strategies. I planned some raps to learn grammatical terms, some games to play in class to test the articles of speech, and a rap competition at the end of the semester.

After planning, I walked past the dining room into the large kitchen, asking Fati if she needed help. She said no, and I wandered off to the bookshelf. Maybe, I would read a good book. I picked up one Christian narrative that seemed exciting and sat down on the wicker couch to read. But as soon as I sat down dinner was ready.

The guys still weren't home, but Mrs. Mensah and I ate together. The guys finally arrived and they had such colorful stories about how amazing Vacation Bible School was that night. When I saw Evans, I whispered that I had saved him a plate of food, and the look on his face was priceless. He was ecstatic. After a minute or two of eating he was called by one of the guys and he was gone once again.

The disappointment that filled my heart was obviously written on my face. What was wrong with me? I decided to sit with the guys around the dinner table although I'd already eaten. They asked how my day was and I told them about how I was promoted to head teacher. I then shared with them how excellent James was as a teacher and how I wished he could be in the classroom. Lastly, I spoke with them about my students not understanding my accent, and we all laughed at that one.

Evans had a distant look in his eyes as I was talking. He wouldn't look at me, and it bothered me. Mrs. Mensah mentioned how Lauren would help me teach when she arrived in a few weeks, and Evans's face lit up!

"Lauren is coming; I can't wait to see her! I miss her; I haven't seen her in so long."

"Who is Lauren?" I asked.

Mrs. Mensah responded, "She is just a family friend…Evans how long have you known her?"

"Hmm it has been about seven years. Eii my sister!" He spoke with such delight of this woman and I saw very clearly that I had no chance competing against Lauren.

Chapter 21

Defeating Self-Doubt: Letting Go of Comparison (and Jealousy)

Jealousy can take root in our hearts so seamlessly that we sometimes don't realize that it is there. By the time you do face the fact that it has taken residence in your heart, it is usually already controlling your thoughts and actions.

Jealousy usually takes root when we compare our life to someone else's life, whether knowingly or unknowingly. Feelings of jealousy can occur to any person, at any age in life, no matter what the person's social or economic status.

I experienced feelings of jealousy when I found out Evans had a play sister that I thought romantically liked him. These feelings were not based on any truth; the feelings were actually more based in fear! I became petty and acted like a person that I didn't even recognize until I made up in my mind to let go of trying to struggle for what I "thought" I deserved. We'll talk more about how to overcome comparison and jealousy after these chapters.

Chapter 22

...And Then Fear

For God has not given us a spirit of fear, but of power and of love and of a sound mind. – 2 Timothy 1:7

When the team of college guys left, I was fearful. They were leaving me alone with Fati and Evans in the house. Yet, I knew they had to go home. Their ten-day mission trip was almost done; we'd had dance competitions, water sachet drinking races, and even chased a chicken. But the fun was coming to an end.

They were deserting me, or at least it felt that way.

Mr. and Mrs. Mensah and Scott, were going to visit their other son in Senegal. Evans was left at the house to take care of me. I gave Scott the biggest hug when he left. Things weren't working with Evans (who seemed to already be in love with some girl named Lauren).

I tried to get to know Scott. But, after talking with him and praying, I knew he wasn't the right choice for me. I didn't feel peace about a relationship with him, but in a foreign country, it sure did feel comfortable.

Now my comfort was leaving. They were leaving me with a man who hardly talked to me, and I was angry and afraid. But mostly, I was disappointed. A part of me had feelings for this mysterious man.

A part of me had been watching him. A part of me knew that something was happening in my heart. I had finally prayed about Evans, and God for the first time told me "Yes."

I kept checking his qualities that I was observing with the list I'd made four years before. Is he mission minded? Is he patient? Is he outgoing? Is he a people-person? Does he want to be a Pastor or Missionary? Am I attracted to him? YES. YES. YES! I had never met a man who I'd felt so much peace with regarding starting a relationship. I was 19 and I had never dated anyone because God never gave me peace about other men who'd tried to date me. But this man all the way in Ghana, West Africa checked off of everything on the list. God had given me peace about him and Evans still didn't even talk to me! *God, why would you tell me yes if he's not even interested in me? Take these feelings away if they are not from you. God please take my feelings away!*

The Mensah's assured me that another intern was coming in a day's time, so I wouldn't be alone with Evans and Fati for too long. But their consolation was not reassuring. The lady who was coming was named, Annabelle. She was a friend of Lauren.

The day that the Mensahs and the mission team piled into the van and left was the first time I'd cried since I'd been in Ghana. I went into my room and sobbed. When I had finally gotten myself together I came out to the living room and Evans finally spoke to me.

"I'm going to the market; would you like to come?" He said it so nonchalantly. I had nothing else to do in the house by myself, because Fati was leaving to go home.

"Okay," I said equally nonchalantly. As we put our shoes on to go to the market, I felt a giddy excitement come over me. I kept telling myself that I didn't like him and I started to believe it after the trip to the market.

I did not yet know my way around the market so I had to be led by Evans which bothered me. Deep down inside I wanted him to know I didn't need him to get around, and that I was perfectly capable. On the dusty red path from the house to the main road he began walking quickly, and the entire time he walked in front of me. I felt like a small duckling following her mother; it was degrading and embarrassing and I was boiling. Who did this man think that he was? Not talking to me, treating me like a child; he was not even trying to make conversation with me!

My pride was broken; but I would show him. I would show this African man who obviously fit all of the stereotypes I'd heard about. He was a chauvinist who didn't want to talk to me because he thought I was below him.

Thankfully, we met friends in town and I didn't feel completely alone because they walked with us back home from the market. Amy and Giftee were both around my age and we related with one another as best as we could, being from different countries.

Evans was surprised that I already knew Amy. I had met her in the hair salon when I was getting my braids taken out a few days before. But this little encounter made me feel much better knowing that I didn't need him to meet people in town. I could and would do it by myself.

That night I ate with Evans, only because there was no one else to eat with in the house. Earlier, I'd seen him reading a book about Martin Luther King Jr., which interested me. Little did I know where that fateful conversation about Martin Luther King Jr. would lead.

Chapter 23

Conversation #1

"You know my students didn't even know who Martin Luther King Jr. was. Did you learn about him in school here in Ghana?"

"No, that's why I was interested in the book. I didn't know how important he was in the Civil Rights Movement in the States. But, you know, I think I would count him as one of my heroes now after reading about him. He stood for equality and loved the Lord with all of his heart. Many of the freedom movements here in Africa were modeled after the Civil Rights Movements happening with Black people in the States. Did you know that Martin Luther actually came here to Ghana?"

"No, I didn't."

He spoke up again, "I only wish African Americans were still like they were back then."

My throat tightened. "What do you mean by that? There are plenty of amazing Black people who have carried on MLK's legacy. And you know MLK wasn't perfect. He cheated on his wife."

"No, it seems like all that Black women want is to be comfortable, they just want money, but back then they wanted equality and justice…things that really mattered."

I bucked back at him, "There are successful Black people, just look at President Obama. He is doing well for himself and his wife doesn't just want money. She is an educated woman, a lawyer even. I'm also an example! Look at me. I don't want all of those things; I don't care about having lots of money, as long as my basic needs are met. God's calling on our lives matters so much more, and when we are living in our purpose all our other needs will be met."

"Is that why you said you would marry a pastor? You know pastors don't make a lot here…in Ghana at least."

I looked across the wooden table at him. He was attractive… chiseled arms, broad shoulders, beautiful dark mahogany skin. His skin was my favorite. He was a little darker than I was, with smooth skin. No, maybe his eyes were my favorite. He had eyes that could penetrate the soul. Beautiful bright eyes that were a bit lighter than his skin. *Stop! Get it together Jeanette. He doesn't like you.*

I responded, "Yes and no. I just feel like God has placed that desire in my heart. I have always wanted to marry a pastor and to be a missionary since I was younger. I had a dream."

"Like Martin Luther King Jr.?" He chuckled.

I looked down at my plate, hurt. This man hated me.

"I'm sorry, it was just a joke. So that James guy at school you talk about him a lot, what's so special about him?"

I was a little taken aback; this man sure did know how to keep me on my toes.

"Yes, I talk about him because he is an excellent teacher."

"So, you like him?"

Again, his blunt questions and penetrating look surprised me.

"No, I don't like him. He's not my type."

"What's your type? Is James too old for you?"

I looked at him across the round table again. And I wanted to tell him that he was my type. Of course, I couldn't say this, I couldn't be so forward. *Why was he asking me these questions? Did he like me? Why does this matter to him?*

"No, James is not too old. But, I want someone who will pursue me to marry me, but many guys are not there mentally right now. I would really like to marry someone who cares about my culture as a Black American, and who wants to go into the ministry."

He nodded, "Oh okay."

I looked at him, "You know I'm surprised you are talking to me, I thought you didn't want to be around me for some reason. You know a lot of African men are a little bit chauvinistic."

His head perked up, and his eyes sparkled mischievously.

"Oh really, so am I a chauvinist?"

"I'm not sure yet." I barked out. I was angry because he'd ignored me for so long.

I spoke again, "You don't seem to talk to me, so I assumed maybe you were. Most of the African guys I have met in the States are a little prideful and arrogant. I am not sure about you though."

He looked a little hurt. Maybe I had gotten to him. "Well, I am not most African men. I am Evans. It's not fair that you are categorizing me as such. Sometimes we have to let go of our prejudice."

Was he calling me prejudiced!? "Oh! So, you're saying you have to let go of your prejudice against Black American women? Because it sounds like you have some false beliefs too."

He again looked a bit hurt, like he was wounded. Then he said something that I didn't expect.

"Yes, I guess I do need to let go of some of my preconceived ideas, because you are different."

"I am not just different. There are many Black American women who are like me. Maybe the ones you have met only cared about money and comfort, but you can't put everyone in a box."

He nodded, "Well, said."

At this point there was an overwhelming tension that only occurs when you realize the person sitting across the table from you is your intellectual and spiritual equal, a tension that only rises when two people realize that they have met their match…literally. We literally just stared at one another with a newfound amazement. I think we loved each other.

He stood up abruptly, "Can I take your plate?"

"No, No, I can wash it."

"No, but I'm already up." He said, "Let me take it and wash it for you."

I conceded. But I stayed at the table wanting to talk with him more. We'd already sat and talked at the table for about an hour. After he finished washing the dishes, with my help drying the dishes, we sat down again at the kitchen table, and talked for hours. At some point he looked at his phone and the time and I looked at mine, and we realized we had to both go to sleep. But we were both reluctant. Finally, he told me goodnight.

That night, I prayed hard. I kept thinking about the dream I had. Was this man my husband?

Chapter 24
Sadly, I Was *That* Jealous

Annabelle, the new intern, arrived the next afternoon, to my disappointment. I wanted more time with Evans alone to talk. It seemed like he was just opening up, and now another woman was arriving on the scene.

I'd almost forgotten about Annabelle until she arrived. She turned out to be one of Lauren's closest friends at their college. And both Evans and Annabelle were eagerly awaiting Lauren's arrival the very next week. I was dreading it. Who was this girl that everyone was in love with?! I was jealous and I hadn't even met her yet.

When Annabelle arrived, I immediately liked her. She was spunky, and now I had a friend in Ghana. She was someone to share my room and talk with which made things so much better, but one of the first things she asked about was my relationship with Evans.

"So…what's up between you and Evans?" She probed the first night she arrived.

"Nothing is up… I don't think. He's like a brother I guess. We just met a few weeks ago when I came."

Her hazel-brown eyes rolled, and her hand went on her hip, "Well, I know when a guy likes a girl, and girl… he likes you!"

"Really? I don't think so; he thinks of me as his sister, I think he likes Lauren."

"Hmm, well we'll just have to ask him, won't we?"

I liked this girl, she had spunk. It takes a certain type of woman to travel alone and be fearless. Especially knowing you'd stand out! She was blond, with a thin physique, and beautiful long hair past her shoulders. She was athletic, a soccer player actually. I thought she seemed pretty cool.

Chapter 25

Flash Forward: Understanding the Full Story

The sixth time Evans was denied a visa we were devastated. Every time we believed that we would see one another in person, the door would be slammed in our faces. Evans would pay the nearly $200 U.S. dollars for the interview application fee, he would complete the legal documents necessary, we'd wait in anticipation for weeks leading up to his visa interview date and then he would go for his visa interview (required for him to come to visit me in the U.S.) and *every time* we would be denied.

At that time, I started thinking, "What is the point in having the relationship if it was going to be spent hurting so deeply?" We had not seen each other in person for two years, and I was hurting because I thought God told me that it was His will for me to be in this relationship. I thought Evans was my future husband.

It was paradoxical…God wanted us to be together…but not physically at that time, because our visas kept getting denied.

I was so confused and I became angry at God for putting me through the situation. Through that pain, but through that anger I realized that it was okay to be vulnerable with the Lord and to tell Him my feelings (even the anger I felt towards Him) because only He could heal my broken heart.

Now, we are able to look back at that time period of visa denials as God's protection, and as an opportunity to grow in our faith.

Nonetheless, at the time, it didn't seem that way. Looking back, 2013 and 2014 were two dark years for us. I held it together on the outside, but deep down inside I knew that I could not make it without God giving me something to help me hold on; in the fall of 2013, that something was actually someone.

That fall, I met a young woman named Mina who changed the trajectory of my life by simply sharing her story with me and helping me regain my hope again. Mina was from Slovakia, and was engaged to a young man from Angola, and their wedding was a few months away. She too had dated her fiancé (now husband) long-distance for four years.

She was the first person I'd ever met who was in a cross-cultural, long-distance relationship like me; and we just connected. She understood the hardships and pain of the distance. She related with my highs and my lows, she loved me with the love of Christ, and she helped me breathe again.

The hurt I was feeling became bearable because God allowed us to meet.

She helped me to cope by being willing to give her time and share her story with me. Our story would not be the story that it is, without God bringing her into our lives.

Chapter 26
Back to the Story at Hand

At dinner that night Evans suggested that we all begin doing devotionals together. Annabelle was in agreement, and I was out-voted two to one. This began our nightly group devotionals. Evans began, followed by Annabelle and then followed by reluctant me.

Evans was quite the theologian. I was impressed by his passion for the word of God, and his zeal for studying the Bible. I was even more impressed when Anna (as we affectionately referred to Annabelle) told me that she woke up late one night and found Evans praying. It was that night that we discovered that Evans woke up every night at 3am to pray!

Our long, late night conversations became a nightly thing. Evans and I could talk for hours. It was only knowing that I had school in the morning and not wanting to leave Anna alone for too long that kept me going to bed at a decent hour.

You could say I was in love, and when the Mensah family came back with their third son, Sean, it was a full house. But Evans and I continued to admire one another from a distance. It got to the point where he'd bring me lunch to school three days every week just to see me during the day. And of course, people noticed.

And those were our two weeks of bliss. It was so blissful that I had almost forgotten that Lauren was coming. But then one day she showed up at our front door, she took the third bed in our room, and I was sour…well actually, a little more than sour.

She came in with a fury with her long auburn hair, beautiful tanned skin, and athletic physique. She truly was beautiful, and I knew I just couldn't compete. I drew into myself. I didn't want to participate in anything she was doing with Evans or anyone else. When she came she gave everyone big hugs. And I knew I couldn't do anything, Evans had known her before I came into the picture, so I had to accept that she was here full force.

"Hey Jeanette, can I go with you to school?"

I almost pretended like I didn't hear the question. If the question had come from anyone else it would have been okay, but it came from her. Yes, her. The very woman who single handedly stole the attention of the love of my life; the golden soccer goddess. She and Evans would practice soccer drills for hours outside in the heat of the day. Then she, Evans, Anna, Scott, and Sean (the third brother) would all do Insanity workouts together. Yes, she was asking to come into my little world at school.

School had been the only thing keeping me sane at that point. It was my home away from home, a safe haven after all of the excitement at the arrival of Lauren. Teaching my students was the place where I felt most at home in Ghana. It was hard work, don't get me wrong, but it was rewarding to see them develop more of a love for learning. I went to school excited to get away from my personal life which seemed to be in shambles. I was in love with my students, the headmaster at school, the little Christian library down the road, the other teachers, and the country. I felt God's still small voice whispering to my soul. *This is home.* I didn't know what to make of those words, but it somehow felt true. Somehow, this was becoming home, or had already become home, or had been home before I knew what home was. The same calling I'd felt as a child, I felt again and again as I walked in town, learned the language, felt the breeze under my skirt. I didn't want to share this purposefulness with her. I wanted it, whatever *it* was, to all be mine.

I heard my voice saying the words before it registered in my brain, "Sure! I'd love to have you come help me at the school."

She proceeded to tell me about how she was also studying education in school, and how she was looking forward to coming with me and seeing me teach. She hadn't even set foot in my classroom, but I was mortified already. What would she think of my teaching style, what would she tell Evans? But then I resolved in my spirit not to worry. I quoted Matthew six softly, "tomorrow will worry about itself Jeanette…tomorrow will worry about itself."

Chapter 27

The Beginning of Forgiveness

For if you forgive other people when they sin against you, your heavenly Father will also forgive you - Matthew 6:14

The next day I woke at 5:30am like I did on most school days and fixed a light breakfast and a little sandwich in a knapsack to take with me to school for lunch. Evans hadn't been as consistent in bringing me lunch to school now that everyone was back. I had a lesson already prepared from the weekend before, and I wouldn't change anything just because we would have a visitor today.

I always carried a forty-five-minute lesson plan and a two-hour lesson plan just in case the next period teacher didn't show up to teach the class. In rural areas in Ghana there is not a system in place for substitute teachers to assist the schools, so if a teacher is absent one day the teacher who had the class period beforehand just continues to teach until another teacher shows up.

On this warm day, I got my knapsack ready, finished up breakfast and prepared my bicycle for my trek. I rode about two miles to school along a little dirt road path every day. I enjoyed taking the scenic route, it was the time that I calmed my little heart and went over my lesson plans in my head for that day. Lauren wasn't up this morning so I figured she had forgotten and wasn't coming.

I travelled out past the gate, mounted my bike, and journeyed to school. My bike ride to school was one of my favorite activities; I enjoyed the breeze through my hair, and the dust that plumed up as I turned and left the gate of the mission house. I enjoyed saying good morning to my neighbors, and to new aunties and sisters and brothers and uncles all around. This morning was not dissimilar to every other morning on my little bike. It was always a bit cooler in the morning than in the afternoon when I would ride home. Cool here in Nkwanta was the equivalent to a hot day in the states; around 85 degrees Fahrenheit was a nice cool morning.

Pedaling hard on the dirt road leading to the house, was an uphill battle. I would then make a sharp left by the entrance to the hospital. Sometimes I'd see friends that I'd made when I arrived walking to town. On market day I'd always pass women with heavy loads of fresh veggies, or fruits on their heads in wide wicker baskets. Most of the time I'd pass women carry heavy firewood on their head. After my sharp left at the hospital the road became a little narrower, and bumpier. Now I was passing residential areas. I passed over a little bridge past the hospital. There were plants whose arms and leaves reached towards the little path I rode on, but I learned to avoid these plants as they were prone to snag onto my dresses as well.

Yes, I wore a dress to school every day. And yes, I wore pants underneath so that I could ride my bike to school every day. I had people laugh at me when they saw me, but then people got used to my daily routine. It was important for me to dress well for my students. I wanted them to know that *they* were *worth* me dressing up every day. I wanted them to know the importance of carrying themselves with dignity and respecting themselves in the way that they dressed.

After riding over the little bridge, I'd pass behind three families' homes and dodge a few roaming chickens (or goats) and then I'd almost be at the main road. After taking another slight left turn I'd pass two primary schools and a wide-open area with red dirt, no grass, and a few houses, and then I was finally about to climb the largest hill past the Christian Library where Mr. Matthew kept the books in order, and then I'd be at the main road. I'd turn left again at the main road and pedal for about a mile and finally I was at my little school on a hill.

Mind you, I would be profusely sweating by the time I arrived, so I had to carry a handkerchief, deodorant, and a few baby wipes in my knapsack every day to be intact for my interaction with my students.

After I'd gotten settled at the school, and had prepared my classroom for my students, I was told that I had a visitor. My heart began to beat, could it be Evans? Had he brought my lunch today? I walked out of my classroom block only to be greeted by… none other than Lauren.

I was noticeably disappointed, but I tried to hold it together to be cordial to my teacher assistant for the day. It wasn't that she'd done anything wrong, she had been nothing but nice, but I was so disappointed that she had taken Evans's attention away.

I walked her around the school just as Headmaster Joseph had walked me around the school my first day. I introduced her to the other teachers, and to Headmaster Joseph. And then it was time to introduce her to my students. The first reaction I got was,

"Eii Madam, Is this your friend from the U.S.?"

I calmly replied that she would be helping us in the classroom for the rest of the week, and that they were to treat her with just as much respect as they treated me and Mr. James. As the class copied a KWL (Know-Want-Learned) Chart, which is a graphic organizer which helps students organize what they know, wanted to know and had learned, into their notebooks from the board, I briefed her on what I wanted her to assist me with. Mainly just walking around and making sure all seventy were on task and working. The lesson occurred normally, after they copied, they did think pair share work from their work books, we went over the answers as a class, and then we played a game of Grammar Four-Corners.

As the students excitedly left the classroom, I was pooped! Every time I taught a lesson I put my all into it, making sure everyone understood. After I taught my lesson for the day I felt like I'd just ran a marathon! Have you ever tried teaching seventy 6th graders all at one time!? I didn't know where Lauren had disappeared to, but it turns out she had called Mr. Mensah to come pick her up to go home because the class was done. I had an English tutoring session with students that afternoon, so I couldn't go home, but was thankful to have my safe haven back. After the tutoring session, I visited Mr. Matthew at the library on my way home, and then pedaled my way back. And I was pleasantly *surprised* by the *warm* reception I received back at the house.

It turns out that Lauren had been singing my praises as a teacher since she had arrived back that afternoon! She had told everyone how well I handled the large class that I had, about my command of the classroom, and how amazing my teaching was.

Well, as you can imagine this softened and warmed my hard heart, and I finally accepted her. I wouldn't fight over a man. She could have Evans. I would be okay; just me and my Jesus.

Chapter 28
Defeating Self-Doubt: Tips for Letting Go of Comparison
(and Jealousy)

1.) **Remember That God is in Control.** If God wanted you to have that car, that man, that job, etc. He would have given it to you. We have to remember that what God has for us as His children is for us. Ultimately, those "things" aren't ours anyways. Those gifts belong to God; He just gives them to us to take care of. And we are the only ones who can take those gifts away when we act in disobedience. In order to overcome insecurity that is manifested through comparison and jealousy we have to remember Jeremiah 29:11-13,

"For I know the plans I have for you, declares the Lord, plans for good and not for evil, to give you a future and a hope. Then you will call upon me and come and pray to me, and I will hear you. You will seek me and find me, when you seek me with all of your heart."

Notice how personal this scripture is. Although the scripture was written to the prophet Jeremiah, I believe we can learn about the character of God and how He relates to us from this passage. The Lord has plans specifically for YOU. He knew YOU before you were in your mother's womb (Jeremiah

1:5). The Lord gives us what He wants us to care for while we are on earth when we seek Him first above all else and act in obedience to Him. How spectacular is that!

2.) **Know That Social Media is Optional.** We must remember that everything we see on Facebook, Instagram, Twitter, Vimeo, YouTube, etc. are the best snapshots and edited videos of people's lives. If something on social media is causing you to stumble, then you have the option to mute, unfollow, and disengage from social media. I have had to take several fasts from social media in the past, in order to re-focus on Jesus being my creator, savior, and primary giver of my identity. We cannot put our self-worth in "likes" or "follows" on social media. Our sole judge must be God. Ask yourself these questions: "Am I pleasing God in this season of my life?" and "Am I obeying God in this season?" If you answered "Yes" to these questions then everything else will be added (Matthew 6:33).

3.) **God Made You Exactly How You Are for a Reason.** When I was younger, I was not happy with my hair type, my skin color, my height, or my body type. I suffered with poor self-esteem and struggled through the beginning stages of an eating disorder at one point in my teens. I believed that I was not beautiful, and that I would never get married. But that was just a lie that the enemy tried to use to kill, steal, and destroy my ultimate purpose. I never had a boyfriend until I dated my husband! And upon meeting my husband and realizing that I actually was attractive, God started opening my eyes to the reasons that He made me the way I am. I believe **God wants to reach specific people, at specific times with our lives** and if I had been disobedient or tried to change my God given phenotype (outward appearance), I would have missed God's blessings through how He wanted to use me and my outward appearance.

Chapter 29
Back in Accra

Having moved on mentally and emotionally from the idea of dating Evans, I was free again. I didn't give him a second glance (well at least not the version of myself that was in my head). Looking back…I probably still had some affinity towards him, but I didn't recognize it at the time. After a few weeks of daily lessons, I was surprised to find out that school would be on vacation for the Form 3 (8th grade) students to take their end of year exams. I was not asked to proctor, so I had the week off. It also just so happened that Lauren was leaving that week with Anna to go back to Accra. I am convinced that there are no coincidences, but my goodness! I did not expect what was suggested next.

"Well, Lauren since you will be going back with Anna this week and Jeanette is on vacation from school…why don't you just show Jeanette around Accra with Anna?!"

I could feel my jaw drop. My eyes were almost popping out of my head.

"Yeah, that sounds like a great idea," others chimed in. And all I could do was sit there, simmering like a tea pot about to spew. I had no reason not to go…so alas all I could do was squeak out a soft, "Sure, sounds good."

That night I found myself packing for the week-long trip. I was the third wheel getting in-between Lauren and Anna who already had an established friendship and I felt terrible. The two girls tried to include me in their excited conversation about all that they would do while in Accra, but I could tell I'd be a third wheel and I didn't like it one bit.

In the morning we were off. Lauren's dad worked for the U.S. Consulate in Accra, so we had all the perks on the way back from Nkwanta. A personal driver, license plate tags that got us any…and everywhere we wanted to go, *and* an amazing house in Accra. After coming from the town, and getting used to my little bicycle, I was in a state of shock to be back in the city. It felt crowded, and nothing felt right. I said a prayer in my head on the ride back, and it went like this:

"Lord, please send me someone. Lord I am lonely and I just need someone I can connect with. Please Lord, send me someone!"

My prayer was answered the very next morning when I received a Facebook message from a friend from university saying that her dad was going on a business trip to Accra, Ghana. Her dad had given her a surprise birthday gift by buying her a plane ticket to travel there with him! She was writing me to ask if I would be in Accra that week. Of course, I immediately said "YES!" I had just arrived in

Accra and we planned for her to come over to tour the city with Lauren, Anna, and myself on Friday.

God heard my cry of desperation, and my Abba cared so much for me that He provided for me. My God had done exceedingly and abundantly more than I could ever ask for or imagine (Eph. 3:20-21)! That day I was floating on air. Despite feeling like a bit of an outsider with Lauren and Anna, I didn't care! My friend was coming to visit. I made arrangements with Lauren for Bridget's arrival. Lauren was literally so sweet and she said that she and Anna would stay home so that I could take their family's private driver and car and have him take us anywhere we wanted to go in the city! When I heard this, I was beyond excited!

In the meantime, I stuck with Anna and Lauren as much as I could. We went to workout at the American Embassy in Accra, we went to the market together in town, and heck we even went Latin dancing (yes, they have Latin dancing in West Africa). As I journeyed here and there with them, I couldn't help but wonder whether or not she had feelings for Evans. I was trying to push the question down, but one night I just blurted it out.

"Lauren do you have feelings for Evans?"

Then I rephrased my question to try to sound more polite, "No, but I mean, like... would you ever, you know... date him? Or marry him?"

"Eww No, Evans is my brother." She made a face like she might barf.

This whole time I had believed that she had feelings for him, when in reality…she really *did* consider him to be like her *brother!?* I was stunned into silence at the realization that she could consider someone so different from her to be like a brother. It baffled me. My family in the States had always stuck to themselves, and never considered taking anyone else in, like her family had done with Evans when he was a teenager.

This…was radical *Love.* This was the type of love Jesus talked about. This was lay down your life for your brother kind of love, and I was astonished. And then after taking it all in, I realized I wanted to love others with *that* kind of *Love.* I realized that I wanted to serve others with *that* kind of *Love.* And I realized that I was just beginning to experience *that* kind of radical *Love.*

"Jeanette…do *you* want to marry Evans?"

The question startled me. It rattled my bones. I looked up at the girl that I had al*ways* wanted to be. My American culture taught me that I need to be super fit, with long blond hair, and blue eyes to be wanted by any man. And now…maybe just maybe I was *wanted* by *this* man.

"Yes, maybe…I think, I do." With that response the two girls screamed with delight! Lauren was in on it, and she *wanted* to set me up with her brother!

Thursday came and went, and then finally it was time for Bridget to come, and boy did I have so much to catch her up on regarding this new development in my possible relationship with Evans.

Chapter 30

Alone in Accra

The Lord himself goes before you and will be with you; he will never leave you nor forsake you. Do not be afraid; do not be discouraged. - Deuteronomy 31:8

I had so many questions racing through my mind. How did I know for sure that he liked me? Was I getting ahead of God's plan for my life, or was this God's plan? What would my family say? All of these questions were running through my mind. At the time my questions seemed viable, but now I look back and realize that these questions were a bit selfish and self-centered, instead of being God centered.

Bridget and I planned to meet in Cantonments, Accra on Friday morning. When Friday finally came around, I dressed in my cutest outfit for a day out on the town. The journey was delightful. Bridget met me in Cantonments and Mr. Eric decided on a few places to drive us around to visit.

We were living the dream. First, we went to an art museum and just explored the beauty that God had gifted humans the ability to create. How wonderful it was to get lost in art in a foreign land, and to just explore and talk and giggle with a friend. What a blessing it was to have her by my side during a time when so many questions were swarming through my head.

Of course, I told Bri about everything that was (or wasn't) happening with Evans, and she was completely in support of praying and asking God what to do. She didn't tell me whether I should go one way or the other, she just let me express my thoughts and concerns and vent. And my goodness how I need to vent to somebody!

Our conversation went a little like this:

"Bea! I don't know what to do, I really like Evans but is this from God? Or is this just what I want. I just really feel like this is from God. It is amazing though. I came all the way to Ghana just to find my husband!? Is this how God works? I am just confused? How would I even date him? Bea, am I crazy? Is this absolutely crazy or no?"

She smiled and lovingly said, "Jeanette you're not crazy, you're just weighing your options. I don't know what you should or shouldn't do? Do you trust the guy? If you do, and you trust that he is sincere than just take it slow and pray and ask God about this."

"Bea, I have already prayed and feel pretty strongly that this may be my husband," I whispered in the large echoing-art museum.

"Bri, I even had a dream that I was marrying him! I've never felt so strongly about something in my life. But I don't know what to do. I'm...I'm...I think I'm scared...of commitment. I just don't feel ready for this. I don't feel ready for marriage and I'm scared the relationship won't work out. I don't want to get hurt. Every time I trust a guy I get hurt, but what if this time it really is God?! What if I miss my husband!? Can I miss my husband? I'm sure God would provide someone else...right?"

Bri looked at me quietly, pensively and finally she blurted out, "Girl, have fun! You're thinking too deeply about this, if you think this is the right guy then get to know him slowly and guard your heart. With time you will know if it is the right decision. Just relax; you're not marrying him tomorrow."

I nodded my head relieved, "Yeah, you're right, I definitely need to relax. Bri you are so right!"

That advice took me a long way, and I'd give that advice to anyone who asks me what they should do regarding a "budding" relationship that is just beginning.

Pray. Ask God. Listen. And then go ahead and get to know the guy or gal! You maybe be getting to know your husband or wife! Or you may be weeding out the people and personalities that are not for you, so that you can be ready to receive your husband or wife. It's never wasted time when you're diving deeper into your relationship with God and deeper into the discovery of a possible life-mate.

A husband or wife is a friend for life, an "ezer kenegdo" life saver beside you and someone you can truly depend upon until the end of your time on this earth. We are not all called into the ministry of marriage, but to those who are, it is a privilege to be able to reflect God's love to the world by the way in which you love your spouse.

However, we must have a relationship with God because if we don't know how He loves us unconditionally then how can we possibly love another person unconditionally? God calls husbands to love their wives the way that Christ loves the church. And he calls wives to respect their husbands and submit to them the way Jesus submitted to God. Both are challenging tasks, but all things are possible through Christ who strengthens us, when we are called according to His purpose (Romans 8:28, Philippians 4:13).

Chapter 31
The End of Denial

That evening I felt so much peace when we arrived back at the house. Bri was picked up by her father, and I just spent the night excited to see Evans the next day. I wasn't excited about the bumpy drive up to the Volta region, but I was more than ready to see Evans and finally tell him how I felt.

I cannot believe I didn't give him a hug when I left. I could just kick myself for not hugging him. What is wrong with me?! Well, whether he likes me or not still, I'm going to let him know that I like him, and then the ball will at least be in his court. I can handle it if he doesn't like me. It will be fine. I just need to get this off of my chest.

That evening I just pondered the possibility of a relationship with Evans and thought about all the challenges that we may possibly face. The funny thing looking back is that I actually had no idea just how difficult the relationship would actually be.

As Anna and I said goodbye to Lauren in Accra, I felt a tinge of sadness. I had spent a month being upset at this young woman for disrupting a relationship that I didn't even have with Evans. And then it turned out that she didn't even have a romantic interest in Evans at all. In that moment, I asked God to forgive me for my jealous heart towards her. The next morning, we set off for Nkwanta again. Anna and I had to finish our internships with the Mission… and I had to face a giant. This was a giant that I'd been running away from for almost two months.

Chapter 32

Defeating Self-Doubt: Letting Go of Fear

In order to release some of those nasty Self-Defeating Thoughts we have in our lives, we have to let go of fear. Fear is the root cause of worry in our lives, and it is the enemy's tool to keep up from fulfilling the God given purposes that God has for us on this earth. It's like a disease that sucks the life out of every God given idea, every God-ordained relationship, and every thought that would otherwise be glorifying to God.

A few years ago, a neighbor of mine who loved gardening told me about a weed; well actually it was a vine. It was a beautiful flowering vine introduced to our area from Asia. However, this vine, Kudzu, was extremely dangerous to the livelihood of other plants trying to grow in our environment. This weed would start small, and slowly suck the life out of its host. After slowly killing its host plant, it would ultimately become the primary resident.

Fear is a lot like Kudzu. Once it takes root, it starts small and then slowly takes control of its host (you) and soon becomes the primary resident in your mind. Fear can look attractive at first, "it's safe," "it makes sense," "it's reliable," until every root of God's life-giving ideas that spring up in your mind become overtaken by it.

Fear very honestly, could have stopped me from allowing God to work through my life. It could have stopped me from going on that first mission trip, it could have hindered me from listening to God's voice, and it could have closed the door to God's best for my life.

Now, don't get me wrong. Safety is very important. However, *if safety is hindering you from obeying God, then it is actually a root of fear, planted by the enemy.* The Bible says that the enemy comes to steal, kill, and destroy, and if you let him he will steal your joy, he will kill your peace of mind, and he will destroy the best plans that God had for your life. A good friend of mine would always tell me, that I was safest when I was in the center of God's will for my life. How true that statement is! When we are in the center of God's will for our lives, we have no need to be afraid. Romans 8:28, says that "All things work together for the good of those who love God and are called according to His purpose."

Now that we have established that fear hinders rather than helps us (it is a self-defeating thought pattern). How do we get rid of it? Before I answer that question, I will let our story speak for itself. These chapters talk about a few things I did to overcome the fear of entering into a relationship. At the end of the chapter we will discuss some of those key things that were done to overcome fear.

Chapter 33
Facing Fears

Deep in my heart I knew that if I expressed my interest, the relationship would end in marriage. I'd had a vivid dream about it all. And I also knew that marrying Evans would take me away from my family.

I knew marrying him and following God's plan for my life meant letting go of everything I'd known and clinging to a new reality. It meant clinging to a new culture, and a new language, and new customs, and new rules, and I wasn't sure I was ready to let go. I was ready to give everything to God, but I was *still afraid* to let go.

On that bumpy seven-hour ride back to Nkwanta, I was silent. I was silently listening to the Holy Spirit whisper to my heart. *This is where I want you to be. You were created for this. I love you and you are my daughter in whom I am well pleased.* He spoke to my heart in a still small voice. God had this as His best plan for my life and I had to dive in, let go, and trust His leading. In our lives, we are all called to obedience to God. The question is, whether we are listening; and if so, whether we will be obedient to the great things He is calling us to do.

When we finally arrived in Nkwanta again, the first person to greet Anna and I was Evans. This time I gave Evans a big hug and he

114

stepped back a little baffled and embarrassed. I could see the confusion written on his face, but I just smiled, and went to the back of the car to get my bags.

The next week was very similar to that awkward encounter when I arrived a few days prior. I was now freely talking with Evans, joking and having fun with the rest of the people in the house. Evans and I were becoming friends, and it was both awkward and exhilarating all at the same time. But I kept my emotional distance; I wanted to follow the Bible and guard my heart through the process. I prayed daily, "Lord if this is my husband please let him ask me on a date, or something first. I'm not going to make the first move. Lord, you know my heart."

And low and behold...a few days later while talking after dinner Evans told me that he'd like to go on a walk and "talk with me more privately." So, we set the walk for the following day, and I could hardly contain my glee. Finally, finally God answered my prayer. This very possibly is my future husband. And with that thought came so many fears...*what if it doesn't work out? What if he doesn't like me? What will my friends say? When will I see him again?*

Yet, through the flood of fears I felt God directing me; leading me and telling me it was all going to be okay. I had no idea about the challenges we would face in the future (and it's a good thing that I didn't) but through the process God taught me how to let go of fear and trust Him with all of my heart, even if I didn't have a plan.

I was the girl who always had a plan, and that people looked to for guidance. I always knew exactly where I was going and usually I got to exactly where I said I would go. I said I would go to college on a full scholarship and I did, I said I would make the Dean's List all four years and I did.

I was that girl that was just favored everywhere I went and in everything I put my hand to. So, the fact that I didn't have a plan was disheartening, but it also took me deeper and deeper into the bosom of God. The Lord drew me close and told me over and over again that I was His child and that He had a plan for my life that I couldn't even imagine. He was and is my place of refuge, and my very present help in trouble. He was the one who had allowed me to succeed for His glory throughout my childhood and teenage years, and He would sustain me going forward. And now I am a witness with a real live testimony of His steadfast love and faithfulness throughout those two years when I didn't see Evans but believed God for the blessing to be his wife, and when he too, was praying for the blessing of being my husband.

I was jittery at school the next day. As I was teaching I just couldn't focus on the material, I was nervous about our upcoming walk that evening. As a result of my lack of focus, my students were also suffering from "lazy-itis" and "crazy-syndrome" which is just teacher language for, "Self-control, and discipline in the classroom was not the greatest."

This was actually the first and only day that I actually walked out on my students. I literally took my books, my bag, and my belongings and left the classroom because of poor behavior. Eventually a few of my students were sent as "delegates" from the class to apologize on the class's behalf. And of course, I graciously accepted their apology and followed them back into the classroom to finish my lesson.

After the lesson my mind was in shambles. What would Evans say? What if he didn't like me? What if he thought I was too young, and didn't want to lead me on? What if he wasn't the right person? All of these questions and fears flooded me. But in an unexpected turn of events as I was sitting underneath the tree mulling over my thoughts, Evans showed up with his bright smiling face. I gasped, much to my surprise he and a friend had driven the Mensah's truck to come and pick me up from school since it was my last week.

I graciously packed up my material, pushed my bike onto the road for them to put in the back of the SUV, and gleefully jumped inside. It was nice to have a ride from school instead of having to bicycle my way home.

In the car, I was teeming with stories about how frustrated my class had made me that day. I worked myself almost to the verge of tears, and that's when I felt his hand in my hand. Evans had reached his hand back to hold my hand to console me, and that gesture meant the world. It assured me that everything was going to be okay; it assured me that he cared about me, and it assured me that I wasn't a failure at teaching; it was just a bad day.

After we returned home and had eaten dinner, Evans and I finally got to go on our long-awaited walk together.

Chapter 34

Defeating Self-Doubt: Tips for Letting Go of Fear

Well, now the story is getting juicy isn't it! We will take a brief "commercial break" and discuss some of the actions that can help you to overcome your fear; prayerfully these tips will assist you in your journey of liberation from insecurity and self-defeating thoughts:

1.) **There is Power in Prayer**: Prayer is the key to aligning yourself with God's will for your life. John 15:7 says that if we abide in Jesus, and His word abides in you, we can ask whatever we with and it will be done for us. How powerful is that! First, we have to abide in God through prayer and meditating on His word, and then we can come to Him and ask Him for freedom from our fear. Isn't it amazing to know that we serve a God who loves us and wants to see us free from fear which will keep us in bondage? It seems simple, but sometimes, all we have to do is ask. Ask God to take your fearful thoughts away from you.

2.) **The Word of God is a Sword**: In order to fight the enemy, we need to meditate on the word of God. Some scriptures I memorized during my seasons of fear were:

- 2 Timothy 1:7

- 1 John 4:18

- Deuteronomy 31:8

But I would encourage you to make your own list of Scriptures to fight fear in your own life!

3.) **Making a List (And checking it twice, or thrice)**: Okay, so make a list of all the reasons you "Shouldn't Do" what you are afraid of, and all of the possible consequences. Next, make a list of why you "Should Do" what you are afraid of. If the "Should Do" list has anything pertaining to hearing from God, or obeying God's word…then that means you would be acting in disobedience to God if you don't do the thing you are afraid of. **Usually the things that Satan attaches fear to are the very things that will free us and bring us a supernatural victory** in some way.

Chapter 35
That Fateful Walk

Evans asked if I was still free for our walk, which, of course I was.
So, we embarked on that fateful half a mile or one-half kilometer
walk to the chicken farm. For the first five minutes we were both
silent. I kept praying to myself, Lord let it happen quickly, let him
say something soon! I'm not sure what I had in mind…but I just
thought the walk would be smooth and natural. However, in reality it
was very awkward. It was like we both knew what we wanted to say,
but neither of us wanted to be rejected by the other. I was afraid of
him not having the same feelings, and he was afraid that I would not
like him.

Finally, after a few, "umms" and "uhhs" I spoke.

"Evans, I think that I like you, and I could see myself marrying
someone like you. I had a dream about having a relationship with
you, and I had a list. And you check off of everything on the list."

Evans looked a bit confused, "you had a list about what?"

"Evans, when I was twelve years old I began writing a list of
character traits that I wanted in a husband. I have refined that list
over time; I have prayed and cried over that list hoping that God
would send me someone that had all of the traits on this list, who

also liked me. And Evans…you are everything, I mean…everything that I have been praying for."

My words came out in a jumble; it was all a beautiful mess.

But then I looked up into his chocolate eyes. And he looked like a boulder had been lifted off of his shoulders. Evans sighed and was quiet.

I kept thinking: *Why is he quiet? Does he not like me? Why did I even say all of that? I shouldn't have said anything. Why am I so stupid? Why am I so dense?! What if he doesn't like me? He probably thinks I am too young.*

Finally, after I had mulled over these thoughts for ten minutes walking in silence. I confronted him, "Do you not have anything to say?! I just spilled my heart out to you and you haven't said a word. Why? If you are not interested in me romantically please just tell me."

Evans responded calmly to my blunt question, "Jeanette, it's not that I don't have feelings for you. What you have said just confirms what God has been placing on my heart. It's just, I thought you liked Scott."

I'm sure my face said it all, "Evans, the only reason I was talking with Scott more than you was because you didn't seem like you wanted to talk to me…at all. From the first day when I met you, after I gave you that hug, you just closed yourself off from me. Scott seemed nice, he was friendly, he *seemed* like he matched everything on my list. But Evans, as I started to talk to him and ask him about his future plans, I realized that we weren't going in the same direction."

We walked quietly for a few more minutes.

And again, I broke the silence, "So this whole time you thought I liked him?!"

He answered quietly, "Yes."

"Evans, I'm so sorry. You were the one I was attracted to at first. Remember I gave you a big hug when I first saw you. I just felt drawn to you. I'm sorry I hurt you. It's funny because this whole time I thought you liked Lauren."

His eyes widened, "What?! No! Lauren is my sister. We grew up together."

I sighed, "Yeah, I realized that when I talked to Lauren about whether she likes you romantically. She said she didn't, and that you were like a brother to her."

"So…This whole time we thought the other person liked someone else."

"Yep…"

We were quiet for a few more minutes. Then I spoke.

"But Evans, there are three more things on my list that I want you to answer. I have been praying that my husband would give specific answers to these questions.

He nodded, "Okay, what are your questions?"

My heart started pounding; I'd prayed for six years that my husband would only want to have one child, which is a rare answer because most people want to have two or three. The second thing I'd prayed for was that my husband would want to go into full-time, long-term ministry in a different country other than my home country (USA), The third thing was that my husband would have an evangelistic heart and a passion for mission work.

From an early age, I knew that God was calling me into mission work, so I asked God for a husband that would help me and would be going in the same direction. These three questions helped me to know that a few guys were not my husband in the past. Some guys said they wanted to go into international business (which was close but not it), some guys said they wanted five kids (definitely not it), and some guys were really close but wanted to do different types of ministry in the USA long-term and that wasn't what I wanted with my life either.

So, I asked him the questions that had weeded out other men in the past.

"Evans what do you see yourself doing in the future, I mean…what is your five-year plan?"

His response was immediate, "I'd like to complete my theology degree in Kenya. And then I want to come back to Ghana and be a missionary to my own people, in the northern part of Ghana. That's what I think God is calling me to do. What about for you?"

I was stunned by how perfect his answer was, he had a heart for evangelism and he wanted to do mission work in Ghana. I answered his question with ease.

"Evans, God is calling me to complete my university degree and to come back to Ghana to work as a missionary/educator in the northern part of Ghana as well. There is just so much to be done in the school system here, and I'd like to see positive change in the education system, especially for poorer kids here in the villages."

It seemed like we were going the same direction, but I tried not to get to excited because I wasn't sure about his views on family...and how many kids he wanted to have.

"Okay, well I know this is a personal question. And you don't have to answer it. But I'd like to know how many kids you want in the future?"

Evans thought for a second, and responded, "Well because of how much I think I'll be traveling in the future for Mission Work, and because I want my family to travel with me, I know it is strange, and maybe you thought I'd want a big family because a lot of men here want big families. But I think I'd be okay with…

Please say one, Lord please let him say one.

…I think I would be okay with just one."

And I almost gasped. That was when I knew. God had answered my prayer of six years with a man who was all the way from Ghana, West Africa.

And then…I threw in the question about sex before marriage.

"Well, what do think about sex before marriage?"

I knew my own stance; I had the biblical perspective and a biblical desire to be a virgin on my wedding day. I didn't believe in sex before marriage, and I prayed that he felt the same conviction.

Evans answered, "Well, I'm a virgin. So, I believe in saving myself for marriage."

"Oh, okay, I'm a virgin too. So, I guess it is a good thing that we have the same conviction."

At this time, we were nearing close to the house, and the close of our walk. I had one more thing that would be the icing on the cake, I'd always prayed that my future husband would take me for ice cream on our first date, without me telling him I wanted ice cream.

Now, I knew this one was a bit crazy, but I was stood up in high school by a guy I liked who told me that he would take me to ice cream. After an hour waiting for the guy at the ice cream shop, I realized that he had left me at the ice cream parlor alone. I was embarrassed and hurt for a long time after that incident and I wanted my husband to...redeem that history.

At the end of our walk, as we were nearing home, Evans told me that he would like to take me on a date when we went back to Accra, before I left Ghana. And of course, I said it would be a pleasure.

Chapter 36
First Date

Our first date was like any first date that goes well... it was absolutely "magical." I wore a red dress that I had made in Ghana while I was teaching. It was the nicest dress I actually had on the trip with me. When Evans first saw me that day, just two days before I was to leave Ghana, he was speechless. He finally mustered up, "Wow...you look so beautiful." To which I smiled and said, "thank you, you look nice too."

Actually, he looked so handsome; my heart skipped a beat when I saw him in his white button-down shirt, with dark denim jeans, and loafers. I was expecting. Hoping that he'd take me to ice cream, knowing that would help me to be absolutely sure that God was highlighting him as a good choice for a husband.

Unfortunately, he took me out to a nice Chinese place. There were no words to express my disappointment. Of course, it was nice, but I had wanted so badly for my future husband to take me out to ice cream on the first date and now what did this mean?

The entire time as we ordered fried noodles with beef and chicken; I wasn't myself. He even noticed I was a bit disappointed and asked if the Chinese food was okay.

"Yes, everything is fine." I responded sourly. I kept an ongoing dialogue with God in my head. *Lord, you know that I have been praying for the "ice cream" sign for three years, ever since that guy left me by myself at the ice cream parlor. You promised me that my husband would take me to ice cream on the first date. God, Evans is obviously not my husband because he didn't take me to ice cream.* Now I laugh at this little dialogue, I had a lot to learn about fruitful communication with God.

And then I heard a still small voice whisper, "Just be patient Jeanette."

So, I tried to relax and be cordial. Although, my thoughts were trying to run away. After sometime, Evans and I finally finished our Chinese food. I was hoping maybe the restaurant sold ice cream, but I looked at the menu again and they didn't. There was no hope of him ordering ice cream to "redeem" the date.

So, he paid and I moped sadly out of the restaurant. I was angry. I was angry at God, and angry at myself for being so naïve, and easily excited.

As we were walking, I felt the Lord telling me to wait. Not to be so easily discouraged. I felt Him say, "Be patient." As those words were re-sounding in my spirit, and as I was moping along, Evans suddenly had an idea.

"Hey J," as he affectionately had started calling me, "Hey J, let's go to get ice cream. I don't really like ice cream that much, but I know you like sweets."

In that moment, my heart fell to the floor. God had heard my prayer and answered in the most extravagant way possible. I got a nice meal and ice cream all on the first date, and I knew in my spirit that this was confirmation. This man…was my husband.

I had grown gravely quiet. I was beginning to realize the gravity of this realization.

I was going to live in Ghana one day. I was going to have to leave my family and home country and learn his language. I was about to go back to the United States in exactly two days, and I was leaving my future husband behind. We would be five thousand miles apart. How was I going to do this? And a still small voice whispered, *"You can't do it, but I can."* The gravity of those words still lingers with me today.

Those words were right. I couldn't do it. There were countless times, over the course of the first two years we courted cross-continent that I would want to give up. There would be moments where I wouldn't see God's hand. And there would be moments I would even question God, but through the process, God's grace would be sufficient enough for me.

Chapter 37

Leaving Ghana: The Airplane

And blessed is she who believed that there would be a fulfillment of what was spoken to her from the Lord - Luke 1:45

You sit on the plane, unable to think complete thoughts about what has just occurred. *What have I just left behind?* The man beside you smiles and introduces himself, "Hello, my name is…"

You hold out your rough hand, "My name is Jeanette." You force the little drops forming inside of your eye sockets back. *I am an adult. I cannot cry, adults don't cry. It's going to be okay. Don't cry. Don't cry, don't cry. Be sociable, you're going to be beside this man for 10 hours.*

"Are you from New York?"

"No, I am from North Carolina."

"Wow, do you have a connecting flight?"

"No, my parents are going to pick me up and drive me back home…back to North Carolina."

"Wow, so…how long were you in here in Ghana? Were you visiting relatives?"

You smile, reminiscing on the country that you are now leaving, remembering your fear and anxiety as you flew by yourself at nineteen to West Africa. Your father's cautionary message two months ago flooding your ears. *Don't be like Taken [...].*

You snap back to reality; the man is smiling patiently waiting for an answer to his question:

"Well, I was mainly working as an English teacher in a little village in the Volta Region."

"Wow, how was your experience?" The inevitable tears are pushing against your eyelids…you try not to think about Evans. The one who you are leaving behind.

"It was absolutely wonderful; I hope to come back one day…"

Chapter 38

Defeating Self Doubt: Let Go of Other People's Expectations

Have I not commanded you? Be strong and courageous! Do not be frightened, and do not be discouraged, for the lord your God is with you wherever you go.

– Joshua 1:9

The next few chapters detail the time after I left Ghana. This time was rife with expectation, mine and other people's expectations for me. So, before we continue I'd like to discuss how to overcome other people's expectations of you.

This particular topic is very difficult for most young adults, particularly because children are trained to obey their parents (which is good). However, sometimes it can be difficult to let go of our parents' expectations of us.

Nevertheless, once children finish their schooling and have become young adults who can work, provide for themselves and adequately make "grown-up" decisions; then it is important that they obey God, even if that means not always listening to their parent's advice.

I know, I know, the Bible says, "Honor your mother and your father that your days may be long upon the earth" Exodus 20:12. Yes, you should honor them. However, the Bible also says, "You shall have no other gods before me" Exodus 20:3. Your adult life should not be more controlled by your parents than by God; because then your trust and your faith are in them more than God. Parents are wonderful gifts from the Lord, but **do not allow your parents (or anyone else) to become your idol.**

The transition from having all of your decisions made for you as a child, to suddenly being able to make decisions for yourself, is drastic. The word drastic may be an understatement. For some of us it is difficult to discern the voice of God in our lives because our parents represented the voice of God in our life for so long. When we are adults we no longer are forced to listen to that voice and that can be scary.

My parents wanted me to be a teacher or a diplomat; I went in an unlikely direction after encountering God and asking Him what He wanted for my life to most glorify Him. In these next few chapters we will see how that unlikely direction unfolded.

Chapter 39

The Journals.

Whoever says he abides in him [Christ] ought to walk in the same way in which he [Christ] walked. -1 John 2:6

October 19, 2013

I told my sisters about Evans today. I had a feeling that Margaret already knew about my relationship with him, but this just confirmed it. Clara, my eldest sister, had no idea that I was dating anybody and she was nonchalant and fairly calm about the relationship. When I told Laud and Margaret, they were concerned. Laud, my sister's husband told me, "Well either you are young and dumb or this is actually something serious; only time will tell." I agree with them. Only time will tell.

October 27, 2013

[...] I feel so young around my family. Like nothing I say really matters or holds value. I know my family thinks that I am too young to be dating Evans, heck maybe I am, but eventually the age thing is going to even out. Right now, I am still transforming into the person that I am to become. Now, I'm beginning to doubt myself and everything I feel like God told me.

I know who God has made me to be, and Evans knows who I am. Evans has seen me make silly mistakes and he has seen me teach and preach the gospel, and he has seen me laugh and just talk from my heart, and he has seen me grieve, he has seen me pray; **he has seen** *me*. **Not the "me" that I was, or have been, but the "me" that I am becoming.**

He sees my potential and he is willing to encourage me because he believes in me. He makes me better and I can only hope that I make him a better person as well. I can only hope that he is growing from being in a relationship with me too. I can only hope. I can only trust God and wait until I reach a "legitimate age" to be respected and listened to. But I know that God gives power to the weak and strength to the powerless (Isaiah 40:29).

I am learning that I have to encourage myself. I don't know it all, I know I need to be humble, but it seems like just when I was starting to feel confident in myself, in my power as a follower of Christ and a dwelling place of the Holy Spirit; just when that confidence was beginning to form, people discourage me.

I may not get the opportunity to show what is in my mind all of the time, but Evans has seen that and appreciates that side of me. I am feeling like it's just me and Jesus at this moment.

December 25th, 2013

Today, my dad announced to my family that I was dating a man in Africa.

After an hour of opening gifts under our Christmas tree my dad decided to bring up the very man he ceases to believe exists… Evans.

"Oh, let's see whose gift came from the farthest away."

Of course, everyone looks around and I say, "Dad I got your gift shipped in all the way from a hat shop in San Diego, I think that is the farthest."

"Oh well what about the gifts you received from Kenya?"

I freeze, all eyes in the room are on me including my grandmother who has constantly been badgering my mother about me "talking to some man" and my aunt and uncle who have no idea that I have been dating a man in a long-distance relationship.

"Well…" I clear my throat, "I am dating a man from Ghana, his name is Evans."

December 27th, 2013

I went to see a new movie, but all I can think about is him; how I wish I could touch his face and tell him it's going to be okay and that we will be together one day. One day doesn't seem soon enough, I want it to be tomorrow. I think back to my time in Ghana.

"I don't have a house, I don't have a car, I don't have anything...but tomorrow by this time God will make a way, tomorrow by this time and God will make a way."

Fati teaches me the words to this traditional Ghanaian song, and I begin to dance around the couch singing along with her, swaying my head, and my hips just dancing freely, full of joy "God will make a way, tomorrow by this time, God will make a way."

February 16, 2014

I miss him. Sometimes tears will come randomly, like when I'm in a meeting, or in class, or talking with a friend, and I have to close my eyes and remind myself that I'm in public.

People are not supposed to cry in public, and I know that I cannot cry because I would not be able to explain my tears, or the situation that I am in to anyone.

But sometimes I just need someone to truly understand and allow me to cry. I can't cry to my family because they don't understand the depth of my love for Evans. And, how could they? They haven't met him and they haven't seen us together.

April 4, 2014

My parents are neutral towards my relationship with Evans. They seem to be neither for nor against Evans. They simply have not met him. My mother takes a very political stance about Evans, but sometimes I just want her to be my mother. I want her to feel with me, and cry when I cry and laugh when I laugh and just feel my love for this man who is 5,000 miles away.

Sometimes I just want her to rejoice when I rejoice and I want her to trust that she raised me to be a woman after God's own heart. I want her to know that I have chosen a man that she will soon come to know and love. I want her to take my decisions seriously and know that although I am young, she has taught me well. I listened to and heard the advice that she had been giving me for 20 years, and she can trust the decisions that I make as if she were making them herself.

She is my mother and she is the only woman who can fill that role.

December 25, 2014

I know that the person at the end of that phone line is worth any trial or tribulation I may have to endure. I am just young enough to still hope; I still have faith that God orchestrated our meeting and He will see it through until the end when we are together doing ministry together and living life as husband and wife.

I know that even when our phone calls drop more than six times in our one-hour phone conversation, it is still worth it to hear his voice for just one minute. I know that God orchestrated our meeting, but it was my choice to say "yes" or "no" to this man, to the long-distance relationship, and the hardships that brings. I said "yes" because I knew that if I said no, I would regret that choice for the rest of my life.

Chapter 40

Defeating Self-Doubt: Tips for Letting Go of Other People's Expectations

1.) As a young adult you have to **discern the voice of God for yourself**. You have to develop your own relationship with God in order to be able to hear the voice of God. In order to develop your relationship with God you need time talking with God and listening to His still small voice through impressions that the Holy Spirit will give to you. This is the most precious relationship that you can develop in your lifetime. God will never leave you nor will he ever forsake you; He will always lead you when you ask and He will never fail you. When friends, spouses, loved ones, family and anyone else fails you, you will always be able to depend on the Lord. God will give you joy despite difficulty, peace that never runs dry, and strength that only He could give.

2.) With that being said, it is important to **release the expectations that other people (including your parents) have placed on you**. You are to be led by the Lord first before anything and anyone else. If God is calling you to be a counselor instead of pursuing that law degree your parents wanted you to pursue, that is completely fine.

Do not get bound up in others expectations of you. Living your life based on other people's desires or expectations is like living your life in shackles and chains. You may feel bound to your profession just to please people, but you completely miss God's greatest purpose for your life because you are too concerned with what other people think.

Maybe you're thinking, "If I don't go to medical school, people will think I wasn't smart enough..." My response to that is...that this is your life (not theirs). You are the one that has to live your life. There are too many people who were driven by everything other people thought they should do and when they achieve their goals and everyone else is proud of them they regret their life decisions because they are not truly enjoying the life they are living., If you are unhappy and out of place, it is only yourself that you can blame.

3.) You allowed yourself to be put in to bondage to other people. You placed yourself in their prison, and **you have the key** to remove yourself.

Your parents don't have to live your life... you have to live your own life. And the sooner we recognize how important that fact is, the sooner we can become free of bondage to what they think. Yes, their wisdom is important, but God's wisdom is so much more important. God's plans are so much greater.

We were created to bring God glory, and as Christians our highest goal should be that we accomplish what God put us on this earth to accomplish, so that we can bring Him the highest glory and praise, worship and adoration through our life's calling.

Chapter 41

The Next Three Years

Many people ask me how I survived two years without seeing Evans in person. I could give you a political answer that winds around in circles. I could give you three steps to handling your long-distance relationship or I could tell you the truth.

The only thing that got me through... was the grace of God. I hung on to hope and joy only by the skin of my nails. And there were many moments where I didn't even have those!

Over the next three years, Evans and I kept in contact via the internet, snail mail, and very expensive cell phone calls. We were both in school, so that kept us busy enough to lessen the intense pangs of missing each other. We would have video call study dates and there were days that we cooked together via video. I'd send him shirts and caps with my university logo on them. He'd send me purses from every country he visited in Africa. I had a purse from Ghana, Kenya, Ethiopia, and Tanzania.

I learned how to rely heavily on God for everything, including my emotional well-being. Three practical things that helped me cope with the distance were prayer, journaling and my church family. Honestly, as I look back I realize that I was in the early stages of depression; the only thing that kept me from spiraling downwards was the Holy Spirit. I considered ending our relationship too many times to count. But every time I resolved to "end it" I heard the Lord whispering in His still small voice, "Do you trust me?" God had very clearly shown me that this was a good choice for my husband. Now, would I trust Him?

I remember one incident when I fasted and prayed about whether or not to end my relationship with Evans. This particular fast came right before I was to fly to Evans's graduation in Kenya in 2015. I remember foolishly, yet faithfully testing God's word. I was foolish to doubt God's word but I was full of faith that God would answer my prayers. I prayed this prayer to the Lord,

"God, if this is your will, allow Evans to have a dream about us getting married. And have him tell me the dream without my asking."

I gave God the duration of my five-day fast to show himself through this sign. Day one passed by with no signs. Day two passed by with nothing eventful happening. Day three sped by, and I started to think about how I would break the news to Evans. On day four, during my daily conversation with Evans, Evans mentioned that he had a dream about my dad giving him my hand in marriage. After that conversation I knew that God had indeed shown himself mighty and that Evans was a good choice. So, I hopped on a plane and finally saw Evans in person after two whole years.

After that encounter with him and honestly with God, I knew that God would align everything exactly where it needed to be for us to get married. My parents amazingly agreed to talk with Evans over a video call after I arrived back from Kenya in 2015.

In December of that year my dad gave Evans permission to marry me over a Skype call. And finally, Evans proposed over a video call on the twenty-third of January in 2016. We filed his fiancé visa application soon after the proposal, only to be delayed for an entire year.

I didn't even know if Evans would make it to our wedding. Evans was approved for the visa. Yet, after three weeks the U.S. consulate in Ghana *still* had not released his passport with the Visa for his entrance into the United States. A week before our wedding day we began contacting our government officials to see if they could petition for the release of my husband's passport. God was testing our faith.

Miraculously, after many tears, many emails, and many phone calls, Evans received his passport three days before our wedding. He left the same day that he received his released passport and… *Evans arrived two days before our wedding day.*

On the 15th of January 2017 we were finally wed in holy matrimony. It was a beautiful testament of God's steadfast love and faithfulness.

And yes, every detail...down to the pastor who married us, happened just like my dream.

Afterward

I couldn't possibly end this book without adding more details about what happened after I left Ghana. I give some hints throughout the book about the difficulty that we had trying to see each other again after first meeting in Ghana. Honestly, the story detailing the three and a half years in-between us meeting and getting married could be another book by itself!

As mentioned in this book, during the summer of 2015 I was able to save enough money to fly to Evans's graduation in Kenya. Upon my arrival, I was warmly received by his friends and church family there. I kept hearing about how much Evans loved me and talked about me to his friends and that was a great joy and encouragement.

In 2016 I graduated from university and flew to Ghana to work as a teacher in northern Ghana for a few months. During those months Evans and I *finally were able to court/date in-person.* We also had our traditional Ghanaian engagement ceremony during that time. My mom and dad flew to Ghana to our engagement ceremony and they finally did come around. Now they are very supportive of Evans and our marriage.

After our engagement ceremony I left to go back to the United States to plan our wedding. I worked as a substitute-teacher during that year long time of preparation and waiting for Evans to receive a fiancé-visa to come to the U.S. It took one year for him to receive the documentation to come and we are still finishing up the long, tedious and expensive process.

Our wedding day was such a joyous day with so many symbols of Christ's love for us. Evans came back for his bride, just as Christ will come back for His bride, the church. My story is not one of a great heroine, no, I wasn't that. I was weak, I was wavering and I was foolish.

But I clung to Colossians 1:27 "God holds all things together…" He held me together when family issues seemed insurmountable and I felt I was going to lose my mind. He held me together when sin was crouching at my door. He held Evans and I together despite the separation of five thousand miles and a few time-zones. And I know that whatever you are going through today as you are reading, that He will hold you together.

I let go of a lot during that trip to Ghana. And I am glad that God has never allowed me to be the same since. Ultimately, in order to overcome insecurity, we have to let go of the very things that separate us from the Almighty God.

When we begin to know Him more and trust in Him for everything, we can become secure in the promises that He gives us through His word. God has not given you a spirit of fear, but of power, love and a sound mind (2 Tim 1:7). When you remember that His word can be trusted and let go of anything that is hindering you from fully trusting and knowing Him, you can finally find freedom from insecurity.

Friend, I hope this book helps you in your journey to overcome self-doubt and insecurity. We will never be perfect, but we can use the principles that our Almighty God gives to us in His word to find our identity and complete security in Him.

I love you and God loves you so much more!
Jeanette Walton

www.ingramcontent.com/pod-product-compliance
Lightning Source LLC
Chambersburg PA
CBHW031514040426

42445CB00009B/226